MW00655475

## Adv
## Women Who Spark After 50

I am so grateful for Aleta for making me feel vibrant and valuable as I age. Society in many ways is not kind to older women. This is an inspiring and validating read that makes me grateful for the risks I have taken to carve out a life I love, and she reminds me that it is ok to love it! Aleta helps us to sparkle and invites us not to waste our life and our gifts just going through the motions.

~ Cindy Zauner-Warner,
Author of Leading with Clarity, Connection and Courage: The Secret to Whole Leadership

"Now is the Time. For real."

Aleta writes of the realization that many women find themselves with time: "If we don't pause to think clearly about the time we have ahead of us, our focus may be on our past regrets or current difficulties."

By purposeful refocusing, Aleta calls on us *not to* ruminate on the things that unsettle us, but rather on the vast possibilities we can forge with time for our future.

And yet perhaps because many women have not had the belief that they had time in the past, they default to old narratives of not having time currently. They don't have an intentional roadmap on how to manage their newly discovered available time.

Until now.

Until Aleta inspires women in *Women Who Spark After 50* to embrace their own time—to consciously curate their life.

And to excitedly take the mere dreams of long ago and set new goals, as they journey full on into the next chapter of their lives.

With story upon story, Aleta will share the many journeys women have taken to rise to (their own personal) occasion of triumph.

Women, what are you waiting for?

Dive into Aleta Norris' *Women Who Spark After 50* and learn what will bring you one inspiration after another in shaping your best life yet."

~ Poppy Spencer, M.S., LCPCFL Supreme Court
Certified Family Law Mediator
National Certified Relationship Expert
Licensed New Life Story Coach

Aleta has changed my life in so many ways. She has inspired me to be a better person and has helped me realize that I can still dream my dreams and also attain them regardless of how old I am! Before I met Aleta and read her book, I felt that my life was very mundane, but now I feel rejuvenated!! If you are feeling stuck or feeling it is too late in your life to attain your dreams, this is a must read for you. Her kind heart and encouraging support will help you get unstuck."

~ Lori Choinski, Member of Women Who Spark
Accountability and Friendship for Success
Membership Community

Aleta makes it so easy for the readers to make relevant changes to their lives by encouraging vision and small/mini steps. You'll learn to be your best you and it's a manageable process.

~ Nancy Bowen, Member of Women Who Spark Accountability and Friendship for Success Membership Community

This book is a gem you will refer to again and again! As a champion for all women, Aleta Norris has encountered many women in midlife and beyond who feel disappointed and unfulfilled. She identifies with these women and shows great compassion and empathy for their plight. That is why she wrote *Women Who Spark After 50*. Aleta reminds us we are only "halfway down the runway," and our best years may still be in front of us. Moving us emotionally with her own personal stories and those of other women, she identifies common issues plaguing women in the second half of their lives. But Aleta does not stop there. She offers us specific strategies to propel us forward by focusing our eyes on the future, helping us to develop a plan, and explaining specific action steps we can take toward positive change. Women of any age: read this book, find inspiration, follow Aleta's sage advice, and you will not only live the rest of your life fully and happily, but you will leave a trail of sparks in your wake that will inspire and ignite others!

~ Sandra E. Duclos, Ph.D.
Author, Waiting for Luigi

I am over the top thrilled with Aleta's new book. There is a sense of both wonder and anxiety as I approach these "golden years." Aleta's new book provides excellent guidance to envision the next chapter of my life. I have gone from feeling anxious to finding a sense of hope and purpose. Thank you for this gift, Aleta.

~ Gloria Potter, Member of Accountability and Friendship for Success

# Women Who Spark After 50

## Inspiration to Reinvent and Reignite Your Life for the Second Half

ALETA NORRIS

Copyright © 2020 Aleta Norris
All rights reserved.

Printed in the United States of America

Published by Author Academy Elite
P.O. Box 43, Powell, OH 43035
AuthorAcademyElite.com

Visit the author's website at www.aletanorris.com

All rights reserved. No part of this publication may be reproduced, stored in a retrieval system, or transmitted in any form or by any means—for example, electronic, photocopy, recording—without the prior written permission of the publisher. The only exception is brief quotations in printed reviews.

For quantity orders, please contact me directly at
aleta@aletanorris.com

Paperback ISBN: 978-1-64746-453-0
Hardcover ISBN: 978-1-64746-454-7
Library of Congress Control Number: 2020915894

Editing by Teri Capshaw
Author Photo by Scott Paulus
Jacket Design by Danijela Mijailovic

Although the author and publisher have made every effort to ensure that the information in this book was correct at press time, the author and publisher do not assume and hereby disclaim any liability to any party for any loss, damage, or disruption caused by errors or omissions, whether such errors or omissions result from negligence, accident, or any other cause.

# DEDICATION

This book is dedicated to you, my friend,
a woman who sparks—or one who wants to
spark. Dare to dream of greater happiness, confidence
and clarity of purpose in your future decades.

The world needs every part
of your awesomeness.

# TABLE OF CONTENTS

## PART III: REKINDLE YOUR PASSION FOR LIFE



## PART IV: FAN THE FLAMES



## PART V: KEEP THE FIRE BURNING

# A NOTE FROM THE AUTHOR

When I wrote my first book, *Women Who Spark: 12 Steps to Catapult Happiness, Cultivate Confidence, and Discover the Purpose of Your Life*, I was thinking about women in their messy middle of life. That was on my mind because I had just come out of it. I had survived my more than two decades of raising kids (most of them as a single mom) while running a company. It felt like a never-ending juggling act coaching soccer, driving carpools, trying to fit in workouts, finding time for friendships, and recovering from divorce—all of the things women do when they're in the middle of chaos.

I wanted to write a book to help women who are still *in* the messy middle because it's tough. Two decades is a long time to balance so many demands while fighting overwhelm, fatigue, disappointment, broken dreams, difficult scenarios, and money challenges. It's also common for women to experience various unexpected setbacks, including feeling like they are falling short in any number of areas of life, especially as caretakers. We could all use some help getting through that time.

Interestingly, though, when I ultimately wrote a book for the women *in* the messy middle, I was attracting more women who (like me) were coming *out* of their messy middle and found themselves asking, "What's next?" or, "Who am I?"

These women often have older kids—teenagers or adults—and suddenly realize they're not sure who they are when they're not hands-on with the kids. They have lost a sense of identity and purpose. Or they're tired of their chosen 20 to 30-year long career. I hear things like, "I've lost my spark," "I'm bored," or "My life didn't turn out the way I thought it would."

As I talked with those women, I started sharing a concept: *Lean into an older version of yourself. Think about your 80-year old self. Envision what she looks like. What is she doing? How is she making a difference? How happy is she? Is she confident? How is she interacting with her family? Her grandchildren? How active is she? What is she wearing? How is her health? What has she been doing with the past two, three, or four decades of her life?*

This is when the realization hits, for many women: *I have time.* If we don't pause to think clearly about the time we have ahead of us, our focus may be on our past regrets or current difficulties. We reminisce the bygone good ol' days of the past, dwell on the things we didn't do, or simply allow ourselves to be tired.

I wrote *this* book, because I know you can shine even brighter during the later decades of your life. Keep reading for inspiration to make that happen!

# INTRODUCTION

## Women Who SPARK After 50

In the fall of 2019, I was at a conference when two women stood on stage, holding hands, announcing an initiative they would be working on together. They wanted to bridge the gap between older people and the millennial generation, especially to minimize frustration and confusion. One woman on stage was in her 80s, and one was in her 20s. I was struck by how alive both women were.

This 80-something-year-old woman reminded me of my maternal grandmother. Until my grandma's health deteriorated in her early 80s, she was fully alive. She woke up every day, dressed nicely, put on her make-up, and always had her hair done. After she and my grandpa sold their lifelong retail business, my grandma became busy with numerous activities. I remember her, well into her 70s, serving three terms as an alderwoman for her community and serving as the organist at her church. She also remained socially active in a variety of ways. On top of all that, she was a steadfast supporter of our family and was actively involved in helping my dad raise us after my mom left.

Please, never stop being fully alive.

Many women believe who they are today is pretty much who they will still be in the future. They believe this life they are living today is the one they will always be living. That doesn't have to be true.

Our minds trick us into thinking our entire history, every choice, every chance, every relationship, every kid, every failure led us to this specific moment—and that we will be stuck in the place we are right now repeating the same patterns forever.

That feeling was my own greatest fear during my toughest messy-middle season in my life. It felt like I would never experience full happiness and ease again.

One of my favorite concepts to embrace in life has come to be: *it won't always be this way.*

When women reach their mid-life—most commonly defined as the years between 45 and 65—many of them forget (or never even realized) that women can, in fact, live their best life during their second half: their 50s, 60s, 70s, and 80s.

One of my "aha" moments during my research was when I read an article about women who had reinvented (or were reinventing) for their second half of life. One woman went to med school at age 57. I. Love. This. She dares to believe that she still has enough meaningful years ahead of her to contribute to others and to live out her own dreams.

For many women today, retirement is not even on their radar, and they are not going to watch the world go by as their own mothers did. They want to take on life with a new spark. They want to be confident and visible and alive in the world. For others, "retirement" is an opportunity to participate in, and contribute to, the world in ways they've always wanted to, but never had the time before.

This is in contrast to women who have a mistaken belief: *It's too late.*

I talk to women who, in the middle of their lives, feel disappointed, disillusioned, tired, and even a bit afraid. Sometimes they simply have no idea where to go next or what to do differently from what they've always done. I also talk to women who are living their later decades—their 70s, 80s, and 90s—happier than they've ever been.

I was especially excited, during this book-writing process, to learn from our older role models. Where are they now? What inspires them to live a fully alive life? What was their messy middle like? How did their fears and worries play out for them? How did they persevere?

One thing that surprised me as I researched this topic is the amount of time it can take for women to become a new version of themselves. It can take years to evolve. This is a process you have to take one step at a time, until one day you wake up and realize you are a new and improved version of your younger self.

# PART I

## DID LIFE THROW A BUCKET OF WATER ON YOUR FIRE?

# CHAPTER 1

## Is There More to Life Than This?

*Do the best you can until you know better.*
*Then when you know better, do better.*

~ Maya Angelou

What's nagging at you? Is there some sort of underlying pain dulling your love for life? Do you even know what it is? If not, don't worry. Many women feel the same way. In this chapter we're going to dig deep and discover what's keeping you from feeling fully alive each and every day. This is the first step to design a life that sparks after 50!

Even if you can't quite put your finger on it, there's probably something bothering you—at least in the back of your mind.

Perhaps it's a not-very-great relationship—or no relationship at all. Or your weight has crept up and you're not as healthy and mobile as you'd like to be. Are you tired, unsure of where you fit in the world, or even feel out of place in your own family? Does it feel like you're constantly on a hamster wheel at work?

Maybe what's really bothering you isn't something in your life, but something missing. Do you find yourself asking, "Is this all there is?" Or, "Why have things worked out for everyone around me, but I'm still struggling?"

By the time you're in the middle of your life, it's likely you've seen the women around you having their own challenges. However, it's still easy to fall into a trap thinking that other people have things easier or more pulled together than you do. Keep in mind that while you may have a peek into the lives of other women, they still likely have plenty of private pain you're never going to fully comprehend. It's a big mistake to burden yourself by comparing your deepest disappointments with other women's most obvious successes. (Instead, we're going to focus on the strategic moves that will make your life so much better!)

One of the biggest things I see nagging at women is finances. It's at about this stage in life that harsh reality kicks in, and women start kicking themselves. *I should have spent less and saved more.* Haven't we all said that at some point? And yet, sometimes facing our problems is so painful, confusing, and overwhelming there's a temptation to look the other way and hope things will work out in the end somehow. Delaying getting a handle on finances is a common area of regret.

Another critical area is fitness. You see it all around you—maybe on your self—over time. The pounds creep up and stamina creeps down. How you manage every other area of your life is going to affect this one including your stress level, time management, and your commitment to changing.

Through all of your struggles, I see what you're doing though. You're keeping on keeping on. Right? Because that's the right thing to do. Wake up every day, show up, and do what everyone around you expects you to do.

**Through all of your struggles, I see what you're doing though. You're keeping on keeping on.**

Since you're reading this book, I'm willing to bet you are getting fed up with that old routine. However, merely getting mad won't help you or anyone around you. But reinventing and reigniting your life will completely change your world and inspire others around you.

Creating a plan for the second half of life is about having an eye on your future and deciding who you want to be, what you want to do, and how you want to contribute to the world. It's about getting rid of the nagging feeling that something is wrong or missing.

Now, let's focus on what's happening today so you can start planning for a better future.

We can start by answering three important questions:

1. What is unresolved in your life?
2. What needs your attention?
3. What do you need to do differently?

*For printable, full-page renderings of these offerings, you can download the free PDF "Women Who Spark After 50 Resources Guide" at the Women Who Spark website:*

**www.womenwhosparkbooks.com**

Below is a list of things to get your creativity flowing. We'll come back to these three questions after you've inventoried the situations affecting your life in the list below.

- ☐ I'm dealing with a job loss or divorce.
- ☐ I don't want to get old.
- ☐ I'm a lifelong people pleaser.
- ☐ I'm scared I'll be lost when the kids leave home.
- ☐ My kids are gone, and I have no idea what to do with myself.
- ☐ I'm not sure what I'll do when my career is over.
- ☐ I'm tired of my career and want to do something else. I have no idea what.
- ☐ I'm envious of young people.
- ☐ I feel completely unprepared for retirement.
- ☐ I don't know how to be in this phase of my life.
- ☐ I'm tired of feeling guilty.
- ☐ I am unhappy with how I've gotten out of shape.
- ☐ I have a desire and restlessness to do more.
- ☐ I have a nagging feeling that something is missing.
- ☐ I feel like the women around me are doing better than I am.
- ☐ I have an overarching feeling of "It's too late."
- ☐ I feel trapped in my career.
- ☐ I'm lonely.
- ☐ I'm exhausted.
- ☐ Add something not listed above: ____________ ______________________________

Now, let's circle around and consider each of our reflection questions.

**Jot down your thoughts:**

1. What is unresolved in my life?

2. What needs my attention?

3. What do I need to do differently?

## What Will Your Trigger Be?

What will propel you to take action? When will you wave the white, "I've had enough" flag? As you read the list below, do you notice a trend? All of these triggers suggest a next step that may feel more like a concept than a concrete action. That's because it's important to think about *what* before you propel yourself into *how*.

- ☐ Feeling exhausted? Perhaps it's time to change your daily focus from doing, doing, doing to slowing down.
- ☐ Are you out of shape? If so, you can reinvent your relationship with food.
- ☐ Does the idea of becoming an empty nester scare you? Consider researching hobbies you might want to take up.
- ☐ Lacking enough money to retire? You might think about work you would enjoy doing as you build up a nest egg over the next several years.
- ☐ Do you feel trapped in a difficult marriage? Ask yourself, "At what expense?"
- ☐ Have regrets about things you haven't done? Then become crystal clear about what those things are. Write them down.
- ☐ Are you trapped and unhappy in your career? Begin to explore options and interests.
- ☐ Don't have any friends? Start by finding *one*.
- ☐ Need some interests of your own? Make finding a hobby a priority.
- ☐ Are you overwhelmed by your big house? Begin thinking about downsizing.

As I mentioned above, there is a lot of thinking woven through this process.

That's intentional. It's okay to start by pondering how your life needs to change. For example, one of my friends, Lori, knows she wants to do something different in her career than what she has been doing for 30 years. She has no idea what it will be. But, she does know sometimes the first step isn't to *do* something different. Often, the best first step is to research and explore options. Lori is dedicating one full year to researching and exploring.

Another friend, Lauren, is ready to move from her big house in the suburbs where she raised her family. It's an overwhelming task and the thought of cleaning out 30 years of accumulated possessions is daunting. She knows it's time to start making some decisions and putting a plan of action in place.

Are you ready to be done with feeling obligated to take care of everyone else? Are you ready to focus on your own dreams and the unfulfilled aspects of your life like Lori and Lauren are doing? Are you ready to start asking the questions about what's next for you? Most importantly, are you ready to take yourself off of the bottom of your to-do list and go for it?

If you're struggling to make yourself a priority, I want you to hear me clearly.

Permission granted.

Yes.

You heard me correctly.

Permission is granted.

By whom?

How about granting it to yourself?

Give yourself permission to do something that you want to do. Give yourself permission to put yourself ahead of others. Give yourself permission to say no to some things, to stop taking care of everyone else at your expense.

**Give yourself permission to do something that you want to do.**

Do you have kids, even teenagers and adults, whom you wait on hand and foot? Listen to me very carefully: *They. Will. Be. Fine.*

Do you have a spouse or significant other whose life you make very easy? *They. Will. Be. Fine.*

Do you have a mom who makes you feel guilty when you don't do something exactly her way? Or who you don't call enough? Or visit enough? You guessed it. *She. Will. Be. Fine.*

I've heard too many stories of women who've stuffed their dreams into a closet for fear of what others would say. Or they've put their dreams aside, because others demanded so much of their attention. They think, *I simply don't have time for myself.*

If that sounds familiar, you are giving people permission to take advantage of you. Is that happening in your life? If so, it's time to shift your perspective.

What would you do if you didn't feel guilty? Let's consider this carefully. Check the things below that you *want* to give yourself permission to do—guilt free:

**I give myself permission to:**

- ☐ Sleep an extra hour a day.
- ☐ Go for regular walks.
- ☐ Start a hobby.
- ☐ Fit in time for my workouts.
- ☐ Go back to school.
- ☐ Watch a show I enjoy.
- ☐ Start a business.
- ☐ Write a book.
- ☐ Remodel my kitchen.
- ☐ Put in new carpeting.
- ☐ Install new windows.
- ☐ Ask for help.
- ☐ Tell someone no.
- ☐ Volunteer less.
- ☐ Go on a vacation by myself.
- ☐ Not make my kids' lunches.
- ☐ Not cook dinner every single night.
- ☐ Not do all of the laundry.
- ☐ Not clean my kids' rooms.
- ☐ Not call my mom every day.
- ☐ Not be the de facto babysitter for my grandchildren.

- ☐ Not mow the lawn.
- ☐ Not shovel the snow.
- ☐ Not do the grocery shopping.
- ☐ Not pay all of the bills.

I have good news for you. For all of the things you're allowing to get in your way of available time, you can do something about those things. You can choose to not do some of them, involve your family more, and even hire help.

## What About the Kids?

Let's talk about your kids for a moment. If you still have some at home, they should be doing their part. Yes, I said *should.* Too many moms over-protect their kids from having to do things they don't like.

Kids can start making their lunches and cleaning their rooms while they're in grade school. They can start doing their laundry in middle school (give everyone a hamper in their own bedroom, and teach them), and family members can take turns cooking. And by the time your kids are in high school, if you're still making lunches, cleaning rooms, and doing laundry, you're hurting their future independence. They should be making their own haircut and doctor appointments, among other things. And how about when they come home from college for the summer or are living at home after high school? Put them to work around the house. The happiest kids are the ones who know they are contributing to the family in a valuable way.

Too many moms fuss too much over their kids, trying to win something. What is it? Their praise. Mom of the year? Your own need to be connected to your kids? Satisfying your innate need to be the caretaker?

I'm being serious here. Your kids will be better off if you stop taking care of every little thing. Allow them to grow into independent humans, one step at a time. What if they stomp around? They'll survive.

If you are mom to some adult kids, you might be looking back wishing you would have required more of them. But you know what? Learning is a life-long process. And as moms we can only choose to do the best we know how to do today. If there are things you wish you had done differently, consider talking to your kids about it. But, most importantly, don't let yourself get stuck in the past. Today is the perfect time to take the first step and delegate some things off of your plate. It's never too late to foster independence among your kids and other family members. In fact, they may have been waiting all these years for you to prove your confidence in them.

**It's never too late to foster independence among your kids and other family members.**

Finally, if you're doing things for others because you want their approval, please stop. You're already lovely. You don't have to expend any more of your energy to earn anyone's approval.

## Your Kids Are Not Your Resume

Since we're getting some things straight, talking about what's nagging you, and getting things in order to look into the future, let's get one more thing clear about the kids.

Your kids are not your resume. (And if you don't have them, it doesn't speak to your innate value.)

Sure, you've invested a lot in them. You can love, adore, and sacrifice for them—as you've likely done for years—but they are not your worth. The choices they've made belong to them. If they're doing beautifully, be glad for them. If they're struggling, be available for them. But don't attach their performance to your value as a woman and as a mom.

If your kids are navigating through the world successfully, be mindful of the degree to which you brag about them. Remember that many women have children who are struggling, children they've lost, and children they were never able to have. Be grateful your kids are doing well, and express to others that you're happy for them. But don't go on and on about their resumes of success in a way that is overly proud and boastful.

And, by all means, forgive yourself for your imperfections as a mom. It's easy to look back and *woulda, coulda, shoulda* all over yourself. *I should have spent more time with them. I should have read to them more. I should have played with them more. I should have been more available. I should have been stricter.* You did the best you could at the time and under the circumstances.

## Let's Get Real About the Tough Stuff

While I was raising my kids, I had things nagging at me—and I had triggers telling me I needed to take action.

My biggest struggle in my messy middle of life was navigating divorce—twice.

As a single mom with three kids, waking up every day to do the best I could—perhaps just like you—I struggled as I looked at all of the *happy* families around me.

I felt humbled by my peers who were in marriages that were working—or that they were working at more successfully than I had.

It was the failure of marriage number two that pushed me over the edge.

I spent so much time reflecting, playing the *woulda, coulda, shoulda* game.

What is wrong with me? What could I have done differently? Where did things go so wrong? Have I ruined my kids' lives? Will their future happiness be compromised because of my decisions?

I'm comfortable with the assumption that my kids never knew about my internal struggle.

I don't mean to paint too dire a picture. A lot of things were wonderful and happy and going well. But there was still a subtle nagging feeling following me around. It was enough to keep an easy sense of joy at bay.

Thoughts of my kids and their well-being were always front and center. They deserved the best that I could give them.

Thankfully, I had a conversation one day that helped me a lot.

While sitting on the bleachers on a Saturday afternoon, watching my young son play basketball, I struck up a conversation with the mom next to me, Peggy. I knew her well, since our sons were in school together. At one point I said, "Peggy, you are such a good mom." Without a moment's hesitation, she replied, "No, I'm not, but I'm good enough."

That moment was pivotal for me. I had known for a long time that I wasn't a great mom, given all of my distractions and competing priorities, but I suddenly felt permission to be a *good enough* mom.

Life isn't easy, but choosing to identify and deal with the nagging pain in your life—in healthy ways—is one of the greatest gifts you can give yourself and the people you care about.

**Chapter Highlights**

**Chapter 1: Is There More to Life Than This?**

- Get clear about what is nagging at you.
- What is unresolved in your life?
- What needs your attention?
- What do you need to do differently?
- Give yourself permission to do things for *you*.
- Remember: your kids are not your resume.
- It's not always easy to do the right thing, but it's always worth it.

# CHAPTER 2

## LET'S GET A FEW THINGS STRAIGHT

*"I wish I'd had the courage to live a life that was true to myself and not the life others expected of me."*

~ Bonnie Ware, Top Five Regrets of the Dying.

What happens when you reach a point in life where you find yourself with no future vision? That is the situation my friend Sarah faced after dedicating more than three decades of her life to raising her three daughters while they moved around the country following her husband's big job.

Sarah loved her career when she met her husband 31 years earlier. She continued working when their first daughter was born, but when the next two came, there was too much stress in the house with two intense careers—and Sarah made the difficult decision to stay home.

Sarah thoroughly enjoyed those happy years raising her daughters, but she also secretly struggled with a feeling that she was always meant to do more than take care of her family.

Her husband is now semi-retired, and they've moved back to their hometown, where they originally met.

Sarah reached out to me for help because, as she shared,

> I realized one day I had no idea who I was without my children center stage. I suddenly felt I had no value to bring any longer, and I felt lost. In my early marriage, I made the choice to set aside a part of my life that brought great satisfaction and challenge. Now, I wonder if I made a mistake.

I encouraged Sarah to imagine the potential 30 to 40 years still in front of her—too much time to accept days of uncertainty and a lack of fulfillment. I asked her what she might be interested in pursuing.

She answered quickly: "I'd love to bake!"

During the years raising her kids, Sarah had experimented with cake decorating and making other beautiful pastries and desserts for special occasions. So she decided to pursue an online baking and pastry certificate program.

She is now having more fun than ever before in her life. Sarah's husband, Mark, is 100% supportive of her new passion, and her adult children are happy for her to have a new passion. She said, "I don't know where this will lead me, but for now I love my classes, experimenting in the kitchen, and showering my family with amazing things to enjoy! I am grateful to have found a way to reinvent myself and my future."

Do you know you have a runway ahead of you in life? In a culture where being young is practically idolized, we're led to believe that the highlight of life is your sweet 16 birthday, high school graduation, college, or your 20s. I hope you fully enjoyed those years, but let's make one thing clear: that was only the beginning.

So many women think their lives have never amounted to anything—and then it's over. Before they're even 50. Yet, for many people their greatest success in their life comes after they turn 50.

**So many women think their lives have never amounted to anything—and then it's over.**

What if 50 is only your halfway point? Do you think at age 50 Betty White could have ever guessed she would be cast in a holiday film at age 98? You may have far more time than you ever dreamed.

This book is all about looking at your runway in life to discover the incredible things you might be able to do in all the time ahead of you.

The financial industry has played a role in conditioning us to look at the middle of our lives as time to prepare for a landing. After all, there's an expectation that we will spend about three decades of our adult lives planning ahead and investing money so that one day we can stop working. Retirement age, most commonly thought of as somewhere in the vicinity of age 65, is viewed as an end to productive work years. Instead, I want you to see it as a time to build up momentum to take off—again.

We've been told all our lives to scramble to invest enough money so we'll one day be able to stop working and do—do what? Exactly what we'll be doing is often vague. But our need for meaning doesn't stop arbitrarily at the end of a set number of years defined by the financial industry. Instead, it only becomes more important as we grow and mature. In fact, it's likely the last third of your life when you will make the biggest impact.

The end of the child-rearing years is another significant milestone for many women. For most mothers, the years of actively raising children come to an end between ages 40 and 60. Many women who experienced a strong sense of purpose during those years find themselves floundering when it's time to move on to a new phase in life.

My friend, Angie, knows what it feels like to grasp for meaning after raising children. She's 45 years old and nearing the end of raising her children while juggling her freelance work. She has noticed that, without her on-duty responsibilities as a mom to her children, she is questioning her value. She shared with me that she feels invisible. When I talked with her a while back, she was in a noticeable funk.

I wanted to pull her out of it. I said, "Angie, let's be clear about something. You have a potential 30 to 40-year runway ahead of you to contribute value. Women are productive into their 80s and beyond. That is a lot of time. In fact, it's more time than you have behind you as a contributing adult."

Her reaction? "Oh my gosh, you are absolutely right! I have never thought about it that way."

That conversation invigorated her and snapped her into action.

Angie's first commitment was to find the time to become more active. Within three months, she was training for her first half marathon. With her new focus on taking time for *herself*, even one of her sons noticed. He asked her one day, "Mom, what's wrong with you?" Unaccustomed to seeing his mom make herself a priority, it didn't look right to him. She happily informed him that she is now going to carve out time for her own interests. Does that sound like something you need to do?

Let's think about your overall quality of life. Since you're reading this book, I'm going to guess you are somewhere between the ages of 45 and 65. (If you're older, this book is for you too—it's never too late to get started.) I've seen women at any age within this range imagine that they don't have time to reinvent. They allow themselves to accept the idea that what is happening right now is the way it will always be.

Here are some warning signs you might be falling into that trap.

Do you ever find yourself thinking:

- *I wish.*
- *If only.*
- *Why didn't I?*
- *I feel invisible.*
- *I'm irrelevant.*
- *Something is missing.*

If any of these thoughts feel familiar to you, don't fret. You are not alone. And even better news, you can turn these thoughts around and begin to believe in—and experience—a more fulfilling, purposeful future.

## The Value of Written Life Goals

Let's look at this point in time—our midlife—from a different perspective.

When I was 22 years old, I was on a flight to Dallas where I would be starting my first job out of college. Having grown up in a small, rural community in Wisconsin, I was incredibly excited about my future. In fact, I could hardly believe I was moving to a big city.

While on that flight, I was reading a self-help book—I believe my first one ever. One of the activities in the book involved creating a list of life goals.

That was so much fun. I was all in.

On paper, my future looked amazingly wonderful. And happy.

I would have a successful career, get married (and remain happily married), have three children, become a talented pianist, travel the world, run marathons, stay fit and healthy, nurture friendships, live in a beautiful home, earn a master's degree—and more.

Creating a list of goals makes perfect sense for any of us when we're embarking on our lifelong journey as adults. I've talked with many women who planned their adult lives while in their early twenties. Their goals may have been only in their heads, but they had them.

And the journeys were similar to mine. Most women—though, I get it, not all—were thinking about marriage, houses, babies, and jobs. Some, of course, took the stay-at-home mom route. And some skipped marriage and babies entirely.

Now we're in our 40s, 50s, and 60s. Maybe beyond. If you think back to the list, you've likely accomplished most of those goals. And, without question, you've likely had some of those goals blow up and go sideways.

For example, I did not have two divorces on my list. Nor did I ever imagine the financial setbacks and difficulties that were ahead of me in the messy middle of my life.

My "happily ever after" was not as neat and tidy as my idealistic 22-year-old self authored on paper. Instead, the road was incredibly curvy, twisty, and bumpy.

Some of the goals and dreams I had on my list didn't happen. That's okay, though. I'm glad I had them. Goals and dreams fueled my progress and instilled hope within me. Goals and dreams propelled me into action.

But what do we do when the goals dry up? When the dreams fade or become irrelevant?

## Fast Forward to Today

A lot of women waste their energy beating themselves up for not getting everything right, for not accomplishing enough. They're still looking around to see what everyone else is doing—then comparing. And they're stuck, ruminating on what went wrong.

But our time is too precious to allow ourselves to stay stuck. If you still have two or three or four decades ahead of you, don't you owe it to yourself to have some new goals?

You have time.

You have time to set new goals, learn new skills, launch new passion projects, start new businesses, earn new degrees, and even start new careers. You have time to get to know yourself again.

Let's get started by discovering the beliefs that might be holding you back—and that will propel you forward once you develop a healthy perspective.

## Your Belief System

Are you guilty of thinking any of the thoughts below? Check every box that applies to how you think about yourself so you can start working to overcome your biggest obstacles.

- ☐ *I'm not good enough.*
- ☐ *Who do I think I am?*
- ☐ *I don't have enough time left.*
- ☐ *That ship has sailed.*
- ☐ *I could never do what she is doing.*
- ☐ *That dream is for someone else.*
- ☐ *It's ridiculous for me to even imagine I could ____________.*

Do your answers feel disheartening? That's okay. You *can* make major overhauls in your life. You can reinvent and reignite. You can find your spark.

Your first step is to believe it's possible. Whatever *it* is. We'll spend the rest of this book exploring exactly why that's true.

You've likely spent a lifetime learning to think the way you do. That means you may have to do some serious work to change your perspective. The first step in the right direction will probably be believing whatever you want to do is possible for *someone*. Most things that provide our inspiration are things that someone else is doing. That is our proof it's possible. The next step is to believe it's possible for women like us. And the final hurdle is to believe it's possible for *you*.

I believe you have much left to give. The struggles you've experienced—and even the battle scars you bear—have great value.

What if you can change the life of even one person during the second half of your life? This is not the time to throw in the towel. Right now, today, I want you to start getting your mind in the right place when it comes to thinking about your future.

One of the most critical elements to being able to help others at this stage in our life is to approach it from a healthy mental state. Right now, 30 million women are in this life stage along with you. An incredible number of them have sacrificed their own happiness and identity along the way to please others. If you are one of them, I'm giving you permission right now to stop worrying about pleasing others and start figuring out how you are going to become a woman who makes a huge positive impact on the world around you.

**I'm giving you permission right now to stop worrying about pleasing others and start figuring out how you are going to become a woman who makes a huge positive impact on the world around you.**

At times, simply giving yourself permission is easier said than done. Many women have a history of being depressed or feeling hopeless. I'm not an expert in this area, but I do know this: if women have something to be excited about, that excitement may help make life feel better.

My friend, Ellen, has an inspiring story to tell about rising above her depression. Several months ago, she was suffering from anxiety disorder and depression, something that has been a steady companion throughout her life. Her husband, who had heard about my *Women Who*

*Spark Boot Camp,* suggested that Ellen join. He thought a forward-looking approach to life might help. With nothing to lose, Ellen agreed. Here is what she has to say six months later:

> Before I went through the process of working on me and designing a future I could be excited about, I was a really good actress. On the outside, I smiled and put on a good show, but inside I was just falling apart. In the past, I always felt like I had to do something big for it to matter. I settled into a pattern: I'd set expectations that were too high, and then my fear would paralyze me. I would feel disappointed in myself, and my depression and anxiety would intensify. During Boot Camp, I learned that baby steps are okay! I realize that I can be purposeful with little things. I can get them done and feel satisfaction. I would describe my past self as lost. Today I feel calm, and I am progressing a little bit every day.

Equipped with a newfound belief in herself, Ellen launched Ellen's Childcare Services in Anna Maria Island, Florida, where she and her husband enjoy time away in their warm-weather home. On her Facebook Page, Ellen shares, "Let me watch your children while you have a quiet dinner out, a few hours on the beach by yourself, or cocktails out with friends at sunset!"

Now, back in Milwaukee as the summer weather sets in, Ellen is putting a new idea into play: helping women over 50 learn how to apply make-up. Ellen is, as she says, "really excited about the moves I'm making in my life." While still showing the same level of care for her husband and two adult children, she has made progress in making herself a priority and in discovering who she is and the role she can play outside of being a wife and mother.

Listen, we need for you to be yourself, because you have a unique role to play in the world. You can continue to serve others, but stop hiding yourself in the name of being selfless. Decide what you want for yourself and live!

I'm not telling you to stop caring about others. I'm suggesting that it's time for you to *also* start showing that same consideration to yourself. You don't have to live your life solely to please others. You can live your life on your terms. Put yourself first at least some of the time. Multiple decades is a long time to keep putting yourself on the back burner.

I want you to decide who you want to be as you grow older. What has been whispering to you? What has been nudging you? As you look at what other women are doing, when have you said, "She's so lucky. I wish I could do something like that!"

Are you even thinking about what you *want* to be doing? Will you choose to tune into your lifelong dreams and nudges and yearnings?

Remember Angie? She realized that she was allowing herself to become more and more invisible as her two-decades long on-duty mom role started to diminish. As I mentioned earlier, she began training for long-distance running and found a great passion in doing so. When Angie and I talked recently, she said,

> When you and I talked several months ago, I was depleted. I didn't think investing in myself and making myself a priority was possible. Now I'm energized and I'm showing up in the world again. Things I thought were unattainable—like finding the time for distance running—actually aren't.

In a short time, Angie went from feeling invisible—and without a spark—to feeling fully alive and excited about what else she would create for her three or four-decades-long future She did the work to make it happen.

For Angie, this is a new beginning.

Remember your runway?

Just like Ellen and Angie are using the time they have to discover new passions and find a new purpose in life, you also have time to discover a new direction for your life.

Or, you might use this time to pursue things you already know you enjoy.

That's exactly what Ellen's sister, Karen, did. When she was in *Women Who Spark Boot Camp*, she reconnected with a passion hobby and turned it into a business. She wasn't planning to launch a business, but the brainstorming on one of our coaching calls unleashed a hidden passion from earlier in her life.

During the call, I asked her to share the things that have brought happiness to her throughout her life. As she listed things, she really lit up when she said, "I used to love painting kitchen cabinets." *What?* I said, "Karen, what an awesome thing to love doing. So many people, right now, are transitioning to white kitchens and hiring expensive painting companies to paint their cabinets. In fact, my husband and I just did that."

By the time our call ended she was giddy. Within a matter of days, she had a logo and business cards for "Paint It New by Karen" and ... drum roll please ... her first client.

In a few short months of working to improve her life, she exchanged her depression for a new passion project. When she told me about her first customer, she said, "I used to think there were too many hours in the day when I was depressed. Now there are not enough hours in the day."

Are you encouraged or inspired by Ellen, Angie, and Karen? As you've read through this chapter, what whispers and nudges have you heard in the back of your mind? What is inspiring you? What are you curious about? Where are you letting your beliefs get in your way? What is your first next step?

I had to go through this process too. I'm in the second half of my life, just like you are. After 30 years in the corporate training and development field and raising three humans into adulthood, my new goal is to help women fall in love with the second half of their lives. It gives me something to get excited about when I get up each day.

## Let's Get Real About the Tough Stuff

It is too easy to get derailed. Recently, I read a book called *Mini Habits* by Stephen Guise.[1] He shared a concept that resonated with me: People have been shown in studies to chronically over-estimate their ability to control themselves. He added, "Big intentions are worthless if they don't bring results. For example, I can *say* that I will exercise for two hours every day, but if I never do it, the size of the intention doesn't matter. In fact, intention without action harms self-confidence."

Many women have lost faith in themselves by the time they reach the middle of their life. There are things they never followed through on, projects that didn't go well, and ways in which their dreams didn't come true.

A friend of mine, Susan, was in a tough spot by the time she turned 50. So many things had gone wrong that she had no energy to even look at her runway—and no belief that she could successfully take off for a next season in her life.

She had told herself so many times, "Okay, that's it! I'm going to make myself a priority, find time to exercise, lose the weight, spend more time with friends." Her list was long.

Her biggest setback was that she didn't follow through. She was excited for a moment, and then her real life took over and propelled her back into her day-to-day routine. In time, this destroyed her confidence in herself and her ability to make any kind of change.

She had, as she described it to me, "lost myself in my marriage." She said, "My ex-husband had a demanding job, and I was responsible to take care of the kids and the house. Our relationship was very traditional, and I became resentful over time. Our relationship was crumbling, and I was doing a ton of grieving while in the marriage. I made a choice to not do anything for a long time. Even when I did set goals for myself, I rarely had the discipline to follow through."

When Susan's marriage finally ended, she was exhausted and filled with doubt about her ability to do anything.

Eventually, though, she was ready to think about her opportunities and take small steps. A year later, Susan is getting her spark back. She has found a career she's passionate about—teaching online—and feels content with her life.

Are you in a tough season? Do you feel discouraged and unsure you can ever rediscover joy in life? If so, let's get a few things straight: you have a runway ahead of you, you can change your beliefs about yourself, and right now is the perfect time to set new goals for your future.

Remember, your past does not define you.

I can't wait to see what you are going to do with the time you have!

**Chapter Highlights**

**Chapter 1: Is There More to Life Than This?**

- Get clear about what is nagging at you, feels unresolved, and needs your attention.

**Chapter 2: Let's Get a Few Things Straight**

- You have a runway ahead of you for the second half of your life.
- You can change the beliefs that may be holding you back.
- This the perfect time to create a new list of life goals.

# PART II

## CLEAN UP THE MESS

# CHAPTER 3

## The Sparks Have Dimmed

*If you don't like something, change it. If you can't change it, change your attitude.*

~ Maya Angelou

Have you ever experienced an overwhelming sense of apathy about life? If so, you're not alone. Some of the most successful women I know have felt that way at some point in their lives.

Kate certainly felt that way. When she reached her 50th birthday, she looked up and realized that she wasn't sure how she felt about entering this next phase of her life. What she did know is that she wasn't noticeably happy.

Two of her kids had left home, and her son—who was a senior in high school—was, for all intents and purposes, living his own life. He had a job, was active in school clubs, paid for his own car, and was well equipped to head off to college the next year. She didn't feel needed as a mom any longer. Not in the same way, at least.

Her career hadn't progressed the way she hoped it would, but it was, well, good enough. Her marriage was okay, although she and her husband didn't have the close, fun relationship she would have hoped for at this stage of their life. She had done the best she could to take care of her health, and she felt she still looked pretty good for her age, even if her weight had crept up over the years.

Friendships had fallen by the wayside as she dedicated her time to juggling work and family. She and her sister had never really repaired their relationship after an unfortunate falling out. She also desperately missed her mom, who had passed away unexpectedly five years earlier.

Being a people pleaser, she spent twenty years taking care of the needs and preferences of everyone around her: her kids, her husband, her boss, her parents, her siblings, and even her elderly neighbors.

She was tired.

All things considered, life was not bad, but as Kate thought about it, she realized it also wasn't as good as she'd like. She was happy enough to get by, but, at the same time, she felt unfulfilled.

Kate had no idea what to do about her problem.

Nor did she believe she really could do something about it.

## Welcome to Mid-Life Disappointment

Kate is experiencing mid-life disappointment, characterized by a feeling of—once you come up for air—"Is this it?"

Many women find themselves disillusioned as they reach the middle of their life. Research carried out by the University of Southern California found that women are generally happier than men as they enter adulthood but end up feeling more dissatisfied than men as life progresses. The study further revealed that at about age 48, men's happiness surpasses women's.[2]

Throughout adulthood, it could be that men have had more freedom to pursue a formula of career plus personal interests like attending sports events or watching them on TV, golfing, hunting, or going to the gym. Meanwhile, women often take on the majority of responsibility for taking care of the home, managing everything their kids need, and managing their own careers.

It's not that the men are not helping with some of the home caretaking and supporting the needs of the kids. However, women, in almost all instances, are the operations managers and master schedulers in their homes. Men often receive assignments, doled out transactionally. This is much less emotionally taxing than what women face on a daily basis.

Over the years—365 days a year, seven days a week, 24 hours a day—well, this can end up feeling a bit like Groundhog Day. The repetition takes a toll.

At a certain point, it becomes monotonous and downright exhausting.

As women enter into menopause, which marks the end of progesterone production (the nurturing hormone), they may notice a difference in how they feel about all of those caretaking responsibilities of their lives.

Kate sometimes wished she could leave her life behind and go in search of a new life that felt more adventurous and more fulfilling. With a whole new chapter ahead of her, she wanted to—for the first time in her life—focus on herself.

## What About You?

How are you doing? Are you satisfied, happy, and even excited about your life? Or are you merely coasting by, accepting a mediocre existence?

Do you wake up every day, handle what is ahead of you for that day, go to bed, wake up, and do it all over again? Have you set your dreams on the back burner?

Do you find yourself looking around and comparing yourself to other women, checking to see how your life stacks up to theirs?

Is your husband looking downright boring to you as he has settled into a routine of going to work and coming home to watch TV or putter around the house and yard?

**Do you have a restlessness that you can't silence?**

If you were nodding your head as you read the paragraphs above, it's time to get to work. Let's start by thinking about three aspects of your life: the day right in front of you, the days behind you, and the days ahead.

## The Day in Front of You

As you take stock of where life is right now, it's likely you will lean toward one side of the scale or the other: satisfied or dissatisfied. In addition to the objective, observable, undebatable circumstances of your life, you can also think about your overall emotional well-being. If life has dished out difficulties over the years, you still get to decide how these experiences will affect your well-being.

Some women are more effective in letting things go from the past than others. And some hold on tightly, letting those past experiences adversely affect the quality of their lives on a daily basis. Past experiences can affect your belief in yourself and convince you to sabotage your own future.

When I speak to groups of women, I have them participate in an exercise. They are each given a list of 40 items that could be labeled as difficulties, disappointments, or struggles. I ask each woman to put a checkmark by the items on the list they are struggling with today.

This distinction is important—*that you are still struggling with today*—because a difficulty or disappointment doesn't necessarily have to detract from your satisfaction and happiness. For example, one woman who experiences divorce may let it break her. Meanwhile another woman moves on from a divorce and finds her spark again. In another example, one woman may have experienced a job loss and lost her confidence right along with it. Another may use it to pivot to a new, fresh career—and now she's grateful for the nudge. And finally, one woman may not be affected at all by someone speaking negatively about her while another may be crushed.

The most significant trigger in my life that catapulted me into a very messy middle was two back-to-back divorces in the span of seven years. It took me a while to recover from that experience, but eventually I got my joy back again. My coach asked me at one point, "How are you not a bitter woman?" The thought didn't even cross my mind. Yet, I do know women who have remained bitter and broken. On my checklist, I would no longer identify my divorce as a current struggle. But many women will continue to struggle with their pain forever—unless they choose another path.

I'll share the checklist mentioned above after the next section so you can assess your own struggles. First, let's take a quick look at your past.

## The Days Behind You

Who you are today is a compilation of a life's worth of experiences. You might categorize each experience as positive or negative. Imagine you spent a lifetime collecting stamps. You've been throwing them into one of two buckets.

Your positive bucket is where experiences go that are marked by happiness, progress, achievement, satisfaction, and good memories. These are the things that went according to plan or even surpassed your expectations.

Your negative bucket is where experiences go that reflect your sadness, difficulties, disappointments and struggles.

The positive bucket is easy. If you have these things, if you've been blessed with a life filled with happiness and positive memories, perhaps your sparks haven't even dimmed. If so, you're poised to keep moving into your future on the coattails of a great past. I hope this bucket is beautiful and happily displayed where you can reflect on and enjoy everything that's in it. You may even want to, occasionally, dump the bucket onto the floor and sift through those memories.

The negative bucket? This one can throw a bucket of water on your sparks. And it can tempt you to believe things will never be better than what you are experiencing at this moment. If your life has been filled with an undue share of challenges, you may have found it difficult to bounce back, find your joy in the midst of the challenge, and imagine a spark-filled future.

I am here to encourage you. Whatever has happened in your past, you are the only one who gets to choose your response to those experiences. You are the one who gets to determine what you will do with your future. Now is the time to decide what you will do with the memories in your negative bucket.

**Whatever has happened in your past, you are the only one who gets to choose your response to those experiences. You are the one who gets to determine what you will do with your future.**

Don't let it sit idle. Do not put it in a closet and shut the door. You have work to do here in order to truly find your spark and joy in life.

Before we turn our attention to the days ahead of you, let's deal with that ugly bucket of bad memories. We can't afford to keep anything around that is dimming your sparks.

**Your Struggle Bucket**

From the list that follows, I'd like you to put a checkmark by the things that have happened, or are happening, in your life that you continue to struggle with.

If you've experienced something on the list but you're not struggling with it today, leave it unchecked.

This checklist is also available as a download at www.womenwhosparkbooks.com in case you'd like to work outside of the book.

- ☐ My life hasn't turned out the way I hoped it would.
- ☐ I don't think I'm enough.
- ☐ I have a difficult relationship with at least one of my children.
- ☐ I'm in a difficult financial situation in life.
- ☐ I'm a mom—and I feel guilty about something almost every day.
- ☐ I have a difficult co-parenting situation.
- ☐ I am afraid of what my future holds.
- ☐ I struggle with shame over past decisions.
- ☐ I am self-conscious about my appearance.
- ☐ I have a poor relationship with my mom.
- ☐ I have a poor relationship with my dad.
- ☐ I lost my mom or dad early.
- ☐ I've been passed over for promotions I thought I'd get.

- ☐ I suffer from anxiety.
- ☐ I suffer from depression.
- ☐ I don't have any friends.
- ☐ I am estranged from one of my siblings.
- ☐ I have an abusive spouse or significant other.
- ☐ Someone in my family struggles with an addiction.
- ☐ I've been unhappily divorced.
- ☐ I've had a difficult break up.
- ☐ Mean words from others have destroyed my confidence.
- ☐ I don't have confidence.
- ☐ I am in an unhappy relationship.
- ☐ I have not forgiven myself for a years-ago abortion.
- ☐ I've attempted suicide.
- ☐ I feel hopeless.
- ☐ I suffer from panic attacks.
- ☐ I have an unhappy child that affects my own happiness.
- ☐ I am unfulfilled in my job.
- ☐ I regret not going to college.
- ☐ I struggle to feel happy.
- ☐ I constantly compare myself to others.
- ☐ My husband is having an affair.
- ☐ I'm having an affair.
- ☐ I'm an exhausted caretaker of others.
- ☐ I have a wayward child.

- ☐ I have an overwhelming amount of debt.
- ☐ I can barely pay my bills.
- ☐ I am afraid to speak up in meetings for fear I will say something stupid.
- ☐ I don't have any dreams for the future.
- ☐ I struggle with physical pain others can't see.
- ☐ I'm raising someone else's children.
- ☐ I have an adult child suffering from mental health issues.
- ☐ I've lost a child to suicide.
- ☐ What, me? I don't have any struggles. My life is so good.

If you checked off items on this list with vulnerability and honesty with yourself, I'm proud of you. These are difficult things. It is sometimes easier to be in denial about these things. You have chosen, however, to embrace the truth of your life.

Now, I'd like you to pause to reflect on these checked items.

Yes, stop reading.

Give yourself a moment.

When I use this checklist with a group of women, I gather all of the completed sheets, mix them up, and hand them out again. I want women to look at someone else's checklist. Then, I ask them to switch with someone nearby, so everyone can look at another. Then switch again. And again. We repeat this another three or four times.

Then, I ask for reactions.

Here's what I hear:

- *I didn't realize how many women are struggling.*
- *I hate to say this, but I feel better.*
- *I thought I was the only one.*
- *I can't believe how much I have in common with other women.*
- *I feel really bad for some of the women in the room.*

One woman shared in more detail. She said,

> When I arrived tonight and saw the room filled with all of these women dressed in suits and heels, with their make-up and hair looking so nice, engaged in conversations ... my first thought was, 'I don't belong here.' But now I realize that maybe we are all the same. Maybe I do belong just like everyone else does.

Yes. For all of the times you walk into a room and feel alone, as if you don't belong, know this: you do belong. You are not as different as you might imagine.

We will be talking much more about how your past experiences may be adversely affecting your mindset and your belief in yourself to reinvent and reignite your life.

What about the last item on the list? *What, me? I don't have any struggles. Life is good.*

Time and again, in a room of 100 women, I've never seen that box checked more than twice. As I inventory checkmarks, some women may check as many as 20 or more items on the list.

The most common struggles include:

- *I don't think I'm enough.*

- *I am afraid of what my future holds.*
- *I suffer from depression and anxiety.*
- *I am self-conscious about my appearance.*
- *I am in a difficult financial situation.*
- *I don't have confidence.*
- *I struggle to feel happy.*

The presence of struggle is real. However, it doesn't have to define you. You don't have to accept it as your life calling. You don't have to despair.

There's a quotation I wrote down in my journal years ago: "Despair is the belief that tomorrow will not be any better than today." Isn't that so true? These words, written by American author and speaker Rob Bell, help provide much needed perspective. It always reminds me that so many tomorrows will not remain exactly the same as today.

Whatever you're dealing with, it will not always be like this. You will not have to carry this bucket around with you for the remainder of your life. It may not be easy to leave it behind, but with work on your part—and perhaps with the help of others—it is possible. Can you imagine one day moving to a new home and leaving that bucket behind? Throw it in a dumpster with the rest of your junk. Not planning to move? No worries. Throw it in the dumpster just the same.

**Whatever you're dealing with, it will not always be like this.**

Now, let's shift gears and image tomorrow: your future.

## The Days Ahead of You

The rest of this book is dedicated to making the most of every single day ahead of you. The first step takes place inside your head.

Decide that you want your future to be better. That could mean any number of things. Perhaps you want your life to be more meaningful, more intentional, or more purpose filled. Perhaps you will choose to be more joyful. I like the idea of being on fire.

Decide that *good enough* is *not* good enough.

Decide you're not going to lug that negative bucket we talked about in the last section around with you.

You don't have to know how this will happen. You don't need the playbook. You simply need to know this is what you want. And, you need to remain open minded for the possibilities ahead, as well as be willing to do some work.

As you look ahead, do you know you want more?

And no, I'm not talking about more stuff. In fact, by now, it is quite likely you no longer focus on the acquisition of things. Things, it turns out, don't bring the levels of satisfaction many of us hoped they would.

By the time we reach mid-life, many of us are trying to rid ourselves of the accumulation of clutter. We're yearning for smaller spaces and fewer possessions to manage.

I'm talking about dreams, goals, wishes, and a sense of lifelong purpose.

I'm talking about moving beyond *good enough.*

Do you want to see your dreams materialize? Do you want to achieve a lifelong goal? Do you want to make sure you can live through the end of your life with no regrets for unfulfilled dreams and wishes?

The remainder of this book is dedicated to the reinventing and reigniting of your life for the second half.

## Let's Get Real About the Tough Stuff:

When Michelle Weidenbenner was in her 20s, all she wanted in life was to be a mom. She knew she would finish her business degree in college, but most of all she wanted to meet a man, fall in love, and have a family.

That dream came true. Michelle got married in her late 20s, had two children, adopted a third child, and was in the process of living happily ever after.

The messy middle in Michelle's life started when her son got married.

Before the messy middle, like many women, Michelle was looking forward to her next season of life. As her children moved into adulthood, she had dreams for all of them and for their families. She also had dreams for herself and her husband. She envisioned traveling, doing her own thing, and, of course, enjoying time with her family.

Today, however, Michelle, who is 62 years old, is—along with her husband—raising her two granddaughters who are 10 and 15. She said, "I'm a mom again. I'm back to discipline, curfews, school, driver's training, orthodontist appointments, and after-school activities. The whole cycle of parenting has returned."

What happened?

Michelle's son and his wife are—today—recovering addicts. For years their shared addiction created turmoil in their own lives, the lives of their daughters, and of their parents. Michelle's dreams were altered. She said, "Their story is not my story, but their story has affected my story. The most difficult thing is 'where do you put the anger and frustration?' You don't want your grandchildren to feel unloved or unwanted, yet you hate the addiction. It's knowing where to put your frustration with the situation."

At the same time, when I asked Michelle about the blessings, she was quick to answer, "The blessing is ... oh my gosh ... there are blessings every single day. It's being able to ask my grandaughters questions and watch them and support them and being on the sidelines, seeing their victories. It's the joy of watching them accomplish things they didn't think they could accomplish."

Her son and daughter-in-law's story—while not her own—has opened a door for her to serve a purpose in her life she had never imagined. As the author of "Mom's Letting Go Without Giving Up, Seven Steps to Self-Recovery," she is helping thousands of moms with addicted loved ones by bringing them support, courses, and a community membership where they can learn how to make new friends, find confidence in setting boundaries, and renew their self-love. Michelle found her runway and she has taken off.

She has a story—like many women—that shows us we can rise above whatever circumstance is presented to us. Though our sparks may dim, we can find our runway toward the next half of our life. We can light up again.

## Chapter Highlights

**Chapter 1: Is There More to Life Than This?**

- Get clear about what is nagging at you, feels unresolved, and needs your attention.

**Chapter 2: Let's Get a Few Things Straight**

- You have a runway ahead of you for the second half of your life and can change your beliefs about what lies ahead.

**Chapter 3: The Sparks Have Dimmed**

- Many mid-life women experience apathy.
- Enjoy the beautiful memories in your positive bucket.
- Do the work required to leave the negative bucket of memories behind.
- You can reinvent and reignite your life for the second half.

# CHAPTER 4

## Clean Up the Things That Matter to You

*If your life is a mess, clean it up. Throw away your excuses, sweep the negative people out of your life, fix the problems that you can and pick up the pieces of your life one at a time.*

~ Sonya Parker, author of *Letting Go of Mr. Wrong*

What happens when the chaos of life comes to a sudden stop?

Will you feel relieved or completely lost? Will you love the life you've built or wonder where in the world you're going?

In *Women Who Spark*, I focused on the overwhelm of life, the messy middle. In this book, we're taking on an even bigger challenge: reigniting and reinventing your life for the second half.

The first step is cleaning up.

If you're like most women, you've been on the hamster wheel of life. Many days, for many years, you've been lucky to make it through each day given everything on your list.

When the last of my kids left for college, I finally had a moment to breathe. I paused one day and looked around. I noticed that I had a lot of stuff in the basement, and bedroom closets were stuffed with, well more stuff, that no one really needed.

I also noticed that I wasn't participating in enjoyable activities that were just for me. Not only was I not participating, I had no idea what those activities might even be. I noticed that most of my friends were the parents of my kids' friends—and most of my time spent with them was in bleachers.

Looking around, I realized that I didn't like the paint colors in my house—the very ones that I had loved 15 years earlier. I found that I didn't have one junk drawer in my house, but instead I had about five of them. I also realized that I didn't have a clue how to sit and do nothing. And finally, I became painfully aware that I had no sense of fashion—which explains the steady stream of eye rolls from my daughters over the years.

In short, I had a whole lot of opportunities to clean up areas of my life.

If I had any illusions about reinventing my life for the second half, I wasn't ready to even think about that until I got a handle on the things listed above.

## First Area of Focus

The first thing I decided to tackle was finding a new area of interest, a hobby. I needed something new and fresh after 20 years of a life centered around my kids. I opened up a word doc and titled it "Potential Hobbies." Then I started a Google search. I had no idea dozens of options would emerge.

A funny thing happened. When I started this process—when I began making progress—I immediately felt better. Hopeful. Excited about the fun I would have.

By the end of an hour, I had dozens of possibilities—cake decorating, photography, urban exploration, knitting, sewing, adventure tours, hiking—and I was ready to try a couple on, maybe sign up for a class.

At the exact time I was in the midst of this research, my oldest daughter needed to use my computer for a moment. She discovered my list of "potential hobbies." Let's just say to a young woman with her whole life ahead of her, a document called "potential hobbies" seemed ridiculous. The kids still tease me about my "hobby" research to this day.

I'm not the only empty-nester finding a fresh perspective through new projects. When I visited my friend, Jill, recently, she was beaming as she took me on a tour of her house. The last of her kids has headed off to college, and she has embarked on a room-by-room refresh. This work in progress is giving her a fresh focus—and those new paint colors are gorgeous.

The makeover you decide to tackle could be even more personal. My sister, Sherri, has been an empty nester for a few years, and she decided she needed to tackle the extra weight she has been carrying around, because it was casting a cloud over every aspect of her life.

Or you might decide to eliminate clutter in your life. Earlier this year, I hosted a "Kickstart Your New Decade" challenge. One hundred forty women participated. Without hesitation, the majority of women identified decluttering as their primary two-week challenge as they headed into a new decade.

This is a great strategy to get started revitalizing your life. You can choose a cleaning project to change your approach to life in a positive way. A number of years ago, my friend Christine and her husband decided to move from their family home to a downtown condo. They started by jumping into a year-long project to clean up the clutter. Their number one rule during the transition to a much-smaller space was "There will be no storage unit involved in our future."

What do you need to clean up in your life that will make you feel happier, healthier, and more hopeful about the future? Let's get to work and figure it out in the next section.

## Assess Your Situation

It's time to look around and see what's going on in your life. Take some time to complete the activity below to discover your most pressing clean-up projects.

**Things I Want to Clean Up**

Set a timer for 15 minutes and write down everything that comes to mind. Consider your surroundings, both inside and out. Consider your emotions, your thoughts, and the things nagging at you. Think, but don't overthink it. If it comes to mind, write it down.

If you're feeling stuck, you may want to walk around your house, room by room, to complete this exercise. Observations about your physical environment may trigger emotional thoughts.

What did you discover? How do you feel about your result?

I am amazed what we can get a handle on when we start with a blank sheet of paper and some time on the clock.

Want to take a deeper dive? Equipped with your starting list, you can now take a methodical approach to make sure you didn't miss anything important.

In the Women Who Spark Life Assessment (available for you to take electronically at www.aletanorris.com/life-assessment), you have the opportunity to assess your satisfaction in ten areas of your life and then identify two or three areas you'd like to focus on. For the areas you select to start with, your report will provide you with a list of ten ideas to get you started. I encourage you to pause here and complete the assessment.

The ten areas included in the assessment, and that you'll take a look at as we continue, include:

1. Your relationship with your spouse or significant other
2. Family
3. Friendships
4. Health and Fitness
5. Spirituality, Joy, Peace and Contentment
6. Home and Space
7. Hobbies and Interests
8. Finances
9. Work and Professional Life
10. Mom Role

If any of those areas do not apply to you, simply skip that topic on the assessment.

## Let's Get Started.

Take a look at these ten areas, one at a time. As you read through the next section, you'll have the opportunity to consider how you may want to approach each area of your life.

You will identify each as:

1. Clean up
2. Reinvent and Reignite
3. Neither. I'm good here.

Let's use Home and Space as an example. A clean-up focus might be a decluttering project in your current home. A reinvent and reignite focus might be selling your large home in the suburbs and moving to a small condo in the city.

Or, let's consider health and fitness. Clean-up may be, "I need to shed ten pounds and stop eating sweets every day." Reinvent and reignite might involve completely revamping your lifestyle for improved health and fitness: start eating whole foods, give up sugar and flour, cut way back on the food consumed, begin an exercise program, start sleeping seven hours or more a night, and focus on getting off meds. In other words, reverse a decades-long unhealthy approach to living.

Your choice for each will be subjective—and you ultimately get to decide if an area of your life needs some cleaning up or if it's time for an outright reinvention of who you are and how you're leading your life.

Since this book is focused on helping you reinvent and reignite your life for the second half, the purpose of cleaning up is to get things in order before you roll up your sleeves to tackle the bigger project. It's like when I have a big project to do for work. I typically spend 15 minutes getting things tidied up on my desk and in my office so I can be in the right frame of mind to take on the big project.

Or, let's say you want to improve your image by refreshing your sense of style, including wardrobe, hair, and makeup. It's likely this process will be an evolution that takes place over several years. A clean-up step may involve going through your closet and removing anything you haven't worn for a year and going through your make-up drawers and throwing out any old, unused make-up. What's important is that you create a fresh start for the bigger project.

Okay, let's get started. For each area, I will provide you with some ideas. These are not exhaustive lists. They are simply intended to provide enough context to get you started.

1. **Your relationship with your spouse or significant other**

   Have you and your spouse grown apart? Have you lost site of the joy in your relationship? Do you need to turn your attention to reigniting your connection with your significant other? Are you missing out on the enjoyment of shared interests or hobbies? Do you need to explore new ways to spend time together? Do you have unresolved resentment between you that needs the help of a therapist? Do you need to add a monthly date night? Do you need to stop exchanging harsh words with one another? Or perhaps you don't have a significant other. Do you want to find one?

Is it time to:

- ☐ Clean up?
- ☐ Reinvent and reignite?
- ☐ Neither. I'm good here.

2. **Your family**

How healthy is your family unit? What opportunities can you find to spend more time together or be more forgiving of one another? Do you have tensions that are unresolved, either within your immediate family unit or involving extended family members? Do you need to make family a bigger priority in your life? Do you need to call your parents more? Be more available to your adult children? Or perhaps less available? Are you being taken advantage of by family? Are you a caretaker of a family member? Do you need more participation from other family members?

Is it time to:

- ☐ Clean up?
- ☐ Reinvent and reignite?
- ☐ Neither. I'm good here.

3. **Friendships**

How satisfied are you with your friendship circles? Do you have at least one or two treasured friends? Friends you can talk to about anything? Or do you even have a friend group at all? Have you spent years declining invitations in order to care for your family? Are you unsure how to go back to friends you've neglected now that you feel ready to strengthen that aspect of your life? As you consider your coming decades, do you envision friends playing a significant role in your life?

Is it time to:

- ☐ Clean up?
- ☐ Reinvent and reignite?
- ☐ Neither. I'm good here.

4. **Health and Fitness**

As I've talked with women in their mid-life over the past several years, this area of life is consistently marked by frustration. Are you struggling with your health? Have the pounds crept up over the decades? Have you let workouts fall by the wayside? What about sugar? Still eating too much of it? Are you frustrated almost every morning while you're getting dressed because things don't fit? Are you uncomfortable going out in public? Do you have a cabinet full of meds? Is your doctor constantly talking to you about making changes? Do you live a life that feels too idle? Have you experienced multiple failed attempts to get a handle on your health?

Is it time to:

- ☐ Clean up?
- ☐ Reinvent and reignite?
- ☐ Neither. I'm good here.

5. **Spirituality, Joy, Peace, and Contentment**

As I've worked with mid-life women over the past number of years, a familiar struggle is to simply "be." With the whirlwind of contemporary life, many women put this part of their life on the back burner. Do you need to do a better job of living in the moment and enjoying simple pleasures in life? Do you need to weave time into your day for relaxation and meditation? Are you spending too much time worrying about your future and regretting your past? Is your contentment overshadowed by an overabundance of goals? Are your high demands of others getting in the way of your sense of peace? Do you need to create a cozy nook in your home to relax?

Is it time to:

- ☐ Clean up?
- ☐ Reinvent and reignite?
- ☐ Neither. I'm good here.

6. **Home and Space**

During mid-life, it is common to have conversations related to both where you live, as well as the amount of space you have. Do you still need the big house? Do you love your home but feel frustrated by the amount of stuff you've accumulated? Do you have closets and storage areas bursting at the seams? Are drawers jammed with clutter? Is your home looking fatigued? Is it time for a makeover? Do you simply have a couple of rooms that need attention? Are you considering a move to be closer to adult children and grandchildren?

Is it time to:

- ☐ Clean up?
- ☐ Reinvent and reignite?
- ☐ Neither. I'm good here.

7. **Hobbies and Interests**

   Many women who have spent their adult lives taking care of others, have never given thought to their own hobbies and interests. Instead, life became formulaic: wake up, take care of the kids (and now the grandkids), manage the house, go to work, check on the neighbors, volunteer at school, and, eventually, take care of their parents. Does this sound familiar? Do you have a hobby or interest? Perhaps you have something from your youth or early adulthood that you've enjoyed but put on the back burner. Perhaps you need to develop some interests. Can you add something enjoyable to your schedule, even if only for a few hours a week? Do you want to turn a hobby into a business?

   Is it time to:

   - ☐ Clean up?
   - ☐ Reinvent and reignite?
   - ☐ Neither. I'm good here.

8. **Finances**

   Oh boy, brace yourself for this one. The majority of women and families in mid-life still have too much debt and not enough money invested for their future. If you fall into this category, you are not alone. Many families carry multiple credit card balances, have a large mortgage, and invest too little for their future. If that sounds like you and you're continuing to shop to your heart's content, it's time to get serious. I see many women putting their heads in the sand about this one while experiencing daily anxiety. I want to assure you that you can accomplish a lot over a 10 to 20-year period, but you have to be serious about it. You have to take it on as an initiative.

Is it time to:

- ☐ Clean up?
- ☐ Reinvent and reignite?
- ☐ Neither. I'm good here.

9. **Work and Professional Life**

By the time we reach mid-life, this area of life often presents us with a lot to consider. Are you ready to retire from your lifelong career—perhaps your big job—and do something that feels less stressful and more joyful? Do you still need to work full time for one to three decades, but you want to discover a new career? Have you lost your spark for your profession after two or three decades of doing the same thing? Did you stay home to raise the kids—and now you have to figure out who you are and what you can do? Are you struggling with confidence in this area and feel ill equipped to take on any kind of job or career? Are you stuck?

Is it time to:

- ☐ Clean up?
- ☐ Reinvent and reignite?
- ☐ Neither. I'm good here.

10. **Mom and Grandma Role**

In Women Who Spark, where I focused significantly on the messy middle of life, it was all about being the mom. Now, though, you may have grandchildren in the picture. What role does being a mom and grandma have in your life? How are your relationships with your kids? How much of your day and life will you dedicate to supporting your family? Will you be an on-duty grandma or an on-call grandma? Will your life, for the next two or three decades, center around your family and their needs? Or are you building a life outside of your family relationships and remaining lovingly available for your family when they need you? Do you have some things to shore up in this area? Or is this the time of life you've been waiting for?

Is it time to:

- ☐ Clean up?
- ☐ Reinvent and reignite?
- ☐ Neither. I'm good here.

What did you learn? Do you have some clarity related to opportunities for cleaning up your day-to-day life? What about your future bigger opportunities to reinvent and reignite your life? Take a moment to summarize below.

What do you want to clean up? Jot down a few bullet points to describe what you'd like to do.

1. Clean Up Area #1:
    a.
    b.
2. Clean Up Area #2:
    a.
    b.

What feels more like a reinventing and reigniting focus to you? Jot down a few bullet points to explain your thoughts.

3. Reinvent and Reignite Area #1
    a.
    b.
4. Reinvent and Reignite Area #2:
    a.
    b.

## Let's Talk About Clutter

I mentioned the notion of decluttering in the area of Home and Space. This is a big deal, and we need to explore it further.

**You are embarking on a journey to have an amazing second half of your life. Before going too far, won't it help to clean up the clutter?**

You are embarking on a journey to have an amazing second half of your life. Before going too far, won't it help to clean up the clutter? What are you hanging on to?

Closets, drawers, attics, basements, and even storage units are filled with artifacts collected over the years. Clothes that haven't been worn (or fit) for years, toys from the kids' childhoods, furniture from your apartment, boxes of photos, outdated computers and TVs, old cell phones, childhood collections, musty blankets, boxes of paperwork, old file cabinets filled with unnecessary documents, food magazines that *might* contain wanted recipes, old newspapers, college textbooks...

Are you exhausted?

Prepare yourself for an energizing, inspired, positive, and no-nagging-feelings-present fresh start.

Decluttering is a painful process. It can take months, and even years. I know this firsthand. As my kids neared their college years, I had my eyes set on a fresh start. I knew I wanted to write a book. I also knew I was experiencing a nagging discomfort caused by too much stuff in my house. I didn't want to tackle my book writing project until I tackled the stuff.

You may not approach this quite the same way, but I gave myself two years to tackle the stuff. I was juggling a full-time job, being available for my kids, fitting in workouts, and spending time with friends. I also added steady-progress decluttering to my calendar. One room at a time. One closet at a time. One drawer at a time.

Two years later, I felt better. I even opened up closets and drawers just to look inside and admire the results. When I finally sat down to start writing my book, I felt a peace of mind. I had the emotional capacity to take on a new challenge.

## Let's Get Real About the Tough Stuff

Remember how I mentioned before that you really don't know the extent women around you are struggling? Well, I know that from first-hand experience. I adore my sister, Sherri, and have an incredibly close relationship with her. At the same time, I had no idea how much she was struggling for years. Thankfully, she now has an incredible success story to tell.

"My junior year in high school is when it started," Sherri told me. "I was overall very sad at that time in my life. I didn't connect with anybody to have a good friendship like I saw happening around me with my high school girlfriends."

Late in high school she found herself frequently binging on food before returning to school for sports practice. She says, "Food, for me, became chemically mind altering. Instead of doing drugs, I was using food."

The summer before she started college, her problems with food became even more serious. "I had my lifeguard job at the pool. I was with my girlfriends who very much had the mentality of binging. It wasn't uncommon for us to order large blizzards from Dairy Queen. One day we were eating those when someone said 'You know what we can do? We can just go in the bathroom and throw it up.' That set off my bulimia, which went on for four years. It absolutely overtook me. I couldn't live past that in my mind. I couldn't focus on anything else."

Her addiction to food became so all-consuming mentally and financially that she even ended up dropping out of college. Thankfully, she did find some help.

> I had a close connection with Julie, a woman I babysat for. She was a refuge for me. I'd go to her house to get away. I became very honest and vulnerable with her. I shared with her where I was at. She encouraged me to see a counselor. I did this for two years. We never talked about my bulimia. We talked about my life, talked about losses. It was hugely helpful for me. I gained a lot of victory. I became a Christian. With the help of this counselor, I obtained freedom from the binging, and walked in that freedom for many years.

But, Sherri told me, she never quit needing sugar.

"I was always at some level of need. For 20 years of my life, it was very manageable. I had, what I might call, a normal food obsession, like many women."

Then two years ago she avoided eating sugar for an entire month. "I thought, 'I did it!' That came down to the difference between then and now. Then, my total focus was giving up sugar. A ton of very positive things happened. I lost weight, and I became pain free."

However, when she started allowing herself to have sugar again, her addiction returned. This old problem was back—and controlling her. "I struggled deeply with some level of despair again. I was feeling out of control. It spirals into every other area of my life. I had a well-woman checkup in February. The doctor said, 'You are of the age now. You're overweight. Your blood pressure is high. If you don't get a handle on this now, it's only going to be harder to bring it in as you get older. I encourage you to lose the weight that you need to, start exercising regularly, and get conscious about your nutrition.'"

Sherri left her doctor's office thinking, "How in the world am I going to get a grip?"

Then she came across a group of women on Facebook doing a 40-day sugar fast. She signed up without even thinking about it, but, still, she didn't really believe she could be successful.

Little did she know that decision would lead to her big breakthrough.

This time her quest to give up sugar became a spiritual journey—and that made all the difference, "Even though I've been a Christian my whole life, I never made the connection. I simply needed to trust God's word. His word was all I needed for victory in life."

Now she says that because her journey is focused on her spiritual health, she is no longer obsessing about her weight.

> I am simply trusting God to be my all-filling sustenance. Food is fleeting. It's a lie for women to believe that eating can satisfy. Always on the flip side, we feel guilty. We regret giving in to the temptation. We physically feel awful about what we just put into our body. It's eye opening when your focus is on the emotional attachment to food, and you pay attention to how habitual your patterns are.

Sherri has now gone three months without sugar and says she rarely feels a need to eat because she's bored or emotional. She's replaced the urge to eat with drinking a healthy amount of water. Best of all, she's not only turned her life around but also inspired others.

"I had a friend who said to me right when I started. 'I could never do that.' Then she saw me 60 days later. She thought, 'Oh my gosh, she looks amazing. And she must feel amazing.' So, my friend did it. Two weeks later, she had lost ten pounds."

Are you as inspired by my sister's story as I am? In the next chapter, we'll hear from more women who took time to clean up.

**Chapter Highlights**

**Chapter 1: Is There More to Life Than This?**

- Get clear about what is nagging at you, feels unresolved, and needs your attention.

**Chapter 2: Let's Get a Few Things Straight**

- You have a runway ahead of you for the second half of your life and can change your beliefs about what lies ahead.

**Chapter 3: The Sparks Have Dimmed**

- Many mid-life women experience apathy. You can treasure the memories in your positive bucket and do the work to leave the negative bucket of memories behind.

**Chapter 4: Clean Up the Things That Matter to You**

- When you look around, what do you notice?
- As you assess ten key areas of your life, what needs cleaned up, and what needs to be reignited and reinvented?
- What two areas do you want to clean up first?
- What two areas do you want to reignite?
- Decluttering is a big, almost-universal area for attention. Where will you start?

# CHAPTER 5

## Women Who Took Action to Clean Up the Mess

*I am not afraid. I was born to do this.*

~ Joan of Arc

Action is required to move us from where we are to where we want to be.

You may not know exactly what your future looks like. That's okay. Do you, however, have a dream for the future that feels brighter than your life today?

Maybe you're coming out of the messy middle of your life. Maybe you're still in it. The first step toward your future is cleaning up the mess around you today.

## The Bridge

I want you to imagine that you are standing on a piece of land that represents both your past and present. It includes all of the elements of your present-day circumstances: your level of happiness, sense of confidence and self-worth, job satisfaction, family fulfillment, health, and financial well-being. It's also possible your land is marked by self-doubt, dissatisfaction, and lack of fulfillment. You get the picture, right?

This land includes your past experiences and your present-day thoughts about them. Perhaps you look back on the past with fond memories of these days gone by, or you reflect with some degree of remorse over the loss of the good times in your past. The degree to which you feel dissatisfied will influence how you look ahead to your future.

That brings us to this next element of the land you are standing on. It represents your thoughts about your future state.

"I'll be happy when I ______________."
"When the kids are gone, I'd love to ____________."
"I wish I could____________."
"If only I had_______________."

You remember the good news, right? There. Is. Still. Time.

**Your "I'll be happy when" can come true. Whatever you'd love to do, decide that you'll make that happen.**

Your "I'll be happy when" can come true. Whatever you'd love to do, decide that you'll make that happen. If you wish you could do something, do it. And replace your "if onlys" with action.

Let's call the land you are standing on today the old land. Look around. Is it a bit messy? Or a total disaster?

Perhaps unwelcome circumstances detoured you to this location.

Or, this land you're standing on may represent the place you once aspired to be. Earlier in your life, you may have wanted to cross the bridge to this exact place. It's your previous vision of "I'll be happier when."

Were your earlier expectations for life wrong? Is this place you once struggled to get to failing to provide you with the "happily-ever-after" you anticipated?

I remember my younger self, as well as the younger selves of many of my girlfriends. We *did* want more. Bigger houses, nicer furniture, resort vacations, and the ability to do lots of things for our kids. Little did we know, we were missing out on internal work in our lives.

The artificial satisfaction of those external trappings we were chasing simply couldn't deliver.

I remember a get-away weekend with my husband when I was in my mid-twenties. We were at a hotel on Michigan Avenue in Chicago. One evening, we were sitting in a hot tub with a few people. A gentleman, who I believe to have been in his 50s, was talking about giving stuff away. He was emptying his house, selling it, and getting the heck out of there.

I was so puzzled by why someone would voluntarily give away his possessions, sell his house, and disappear into the sunset with a backpack on his back. I was in love with buying stuff for our new house!

My observation today as I look around as a 57-year old woman—and what I know now about so many of my girlfriends—is that, at this stage, we want less. We want smaller houses, we want fewer possessions—and the irony is, in some cases, we created more mess in the middle because of our quest to have the very things we now don't want to have.

That's okay. This is growth too. "I went after it, got it ... and now I don't want it." This is the wisdom we get with age. It can be embarrassing to learn things the hard way, but it's better to learn and grow than remain stuck and miserable.

Remember my sister Sherri's story from the last chapter? Looking back on this as an adult, it's painful to imagine how casually those young women fell into an eating disorder as serious as bulimia. Now so many years later, Sherri had to be intentional and make a deliberate choice to rise above her lifelong struggle with food. For the first time ever, as a 51-year old adult woman, she has conquered the hold that sugar has had on her for her entire adult life. She crossed her bridge.

Wherever you stand today, there is a bridge to take you away from the old land—if you want it.

While you may not be able to see the other side of the bridge, it's there. What's tricky about the new land, however, is that you don't know exactly what it looks like. You may only have a vague idea of what's there. You may not even know exactly what you're hoping to accomplish. And, worst of all, it may be farther away than you want it to be.

My recommendation for you is to step onto the bridge. Take one step. The most obvious step you can take is to start to clean up the things making it difficult for you to make progress. Really, the first half of the bridge involves tidying up the mess in the old land, both physically and emotionally. This clean up is essential to pave the way for your new possibilities—the ones you'll discover as you make progress across the bridge.

My old land back in 2003 required a lot of clean up. After my second marriage ended, I barely knew where to start. I wasn't thinking about a happy new land somewhere over the horizon, because I was too embroiled in the mess that I was standing in.

I was financially and emotionally devastated. I was putting in long days to manage all of my responsibilities related to my kids, the house, and my work. Emotionally, I was grappling with a lot of regret and beating myself up over past decisions—those that had landed me in that set of circumstances.

I needed to move away from the old land. In order to do that, I put together a detailed budget and managed my finances to the penny. I also made copious to-do lists to make sure I wasn't dropping any balls, I got extremely serious about my work to keep us in our home, and I started journaling.

It took me years to cross the bridge to the new land, where I now enjoy financial security, freedom from regret, a great relationship with my kids—plus two more blessings: a happy marriage to Steve, and a new passion business, *Women Who Spark*.

I want to underscore this: I didn't know exactly what my new land would look like when I started out. I certainly did not have the concept for *Women Who Spark*, which didn't exist until I wrote my first book by the same name in 2019. Things evolve—and that's a good thing.

**Don't let fear of the unknown keep you from stepping onto the bridge.**

## Women Who Stepped Onto the Bridge

Do you need some inspiration to get started on your own journey? I hope the stories below give you hope.

## Angela

Angela was happy with her life as a stay-at-home mom to two kids. She noticed, however, that whenever she attended events with her husband, and others around her asked what she did, she felt uncomfortable answering that she *only* stayed home with the kids. She decided to draw on her expertise from her past corporate days and start her own consulting business. Because her husband has a great job that takes up a lot of his time, she is still first and foremost dedicated to being available to her family. But she has done the work to create an impressive brand—her step onto the bridge—and she is loving it!

## Ellen

You met Ellen in Chapter 2. Before she could do anything, she needed to address her anxiety and depression. In addition to seeing her doctor for the proper medication, she enrolled in the Women Who Spark Boot Camp. That was her step onto the bridge. Prior to this, Ellen had a tendency to set goals for herself that were too lofty—then not follow through. That only magnified her anxiety.

In Boot Camp, she learned the value of steady progress. She decided she would do one thing a day. If she accomplished one thing—baking a cake, doing the laundry, shopping for groceries, designing new business card—then her day would be a success. That concept changed her life. It helped her shift from chronically feeling disappointed in herself to feeling calm on a daily basis.

### Kim

Kim has something brighter in her future, though she is not exactly sure what it is. What she does know, is that she's now showing up in the professional world better. Her first step onto the bridge was to clean up her LinkedIn profile. Now she has a new image worthy of the future she's ready to step into. Whatever lies ahead in her future, she's more confident about pursuing it with a more professional online presence.

### Kate

After a tough decade—for a host of reasons—Kate lost her spark. She isn't the cheerful, happy woman most people once knew, but she's getting closer. She dreams of a happier future in her new land and holds onto hope that she will successfully leave the old land behind. She doesn't have the answer, but she does have a few things staring right at her every day.

She has decided to begin working on her relationship with her husband, quietly, by being more attentive to him. This won't even beg a conversation. She is simply going to do it. And to help support her hoped-for positivity, she is going to declutter one drawer, closet or area in her house every week. She is on the bridge.

### Wendy

Wendy lost herself inside of her marriage. After giving up who she was to make her marriage work, she eventually grew resentful. Ultimately, her marriage ended and, in the aftermath, her mind would not shut off. She was stuck in a pattern of fear and dwelling on the past.

Wendy knew she would not be able to move forward if this didn't change. She also was confident she would make better decisions if she could find peace within. Her first step onto the bridge was to calm her thinking. She began meditating, and it changed her life. She shifted from surviving to thriving. She has since discovered a new career she's passionate about and she is excited about the possibilities in her new land.

## Let's Get Real About the Tough Stuff

My second husband financed a secret life for five years that created an unimaginable financial burden in our life. Because of his variety of addictions—and resulting behavior—I eventually had no choice but to end the marriage.

Talk about scary tough stuff!

I was facing a pile of debt, a big mortgage, college ahead in the distance for three kids, and a credit score of 520. I had a real mess to clean up.

I was on the bridge immediately. I had a budget that was so detailed to the penny that it would not allow a stop at McDonald's on the way home from a soccer game. In addition to continuing to co-lead my leadership development company with my business partner (of now 25 years), I took an extra consulting side job so I could use that money to max out my IRA.

The kids and I went without a lot of things for many years. I know I was more aware of the tough days than the kids were.

Every night, like clockwork, I woke up at 3:00 am, filled with anxious thoughts that I would not be able to pull it off. That sleep loss due to anxiety went on for months.

One of my biggest worries and regrets related to what the kids were missing out on. I remember the families around me having bigger vacations, classmates piling into a bus on Sunday to go to the ski hill for the day, cottages on a lake, ballgames, dinners out, nicer wardrobes, and better cooked meals.

We—the kids were on the bridge with me—crossed one small step at a time. It took years.

An interesting thing happened in the end: my kids look back on their childhood fondly and can't recall that money was an issue. As adults, they are enjoying many new experiences for the first time, contributing to their sense of awe and happiness.

I read an article somewhere along the way recently that said millennials are happier in their adult life if they did not experience an over-indulgent childhood.

Well, there you go. Mine did not have an over-indulgent childhood. Who knew?

Those tough years started 17 years ago. It's all good now, but the bridge was a long, unsturdy, rickety one. I am sure glad to be on the other side.

## Chapter Highlights

**Chapter 1: Is There More to Life Than This?**

- Get clear about what is nagging at you, feels unresolved, and needs your attention.

**Chapter 2: Let's Get a Few Things Straight**

- You have a runway ahead of you for the second half of your life and can change your beliefs about what lies ahead.

**Chapter 3: The Sparks Have Dimmed**

- Many mid-life women experience apathy in their life. You can treasure the memories in your positive bucket and do the work to leave the negative bucket of memories behind.

**Chapter 4: Clean Up the Things That Matter to You**

- When you look around, what do you notice? As you assess ten areas of your life, what areas need to be cleaned up? Which need to be reignited and reinvented?

**Chapter 5: Women Who Took Action to Clean Up the Mess**

- A bridge connects the old land to the new land.
- You don't have to have a clear picture of your new land to step onto the bridge.
- Your first step will likely involve cleaning up a mess.

# PART III

## REKINDLE YOUR PASSION FOR LIFE

# CHAPTER 6

## It's Time to Reignite and Reinvent

*It's never too late—never too late to start over,*
*never too late to be happy.*

~ Jane Fonda

By now, you've done some thinking.

You've reflected on your imperfect life and pondered about what happened to your unrealized passions and dreams.

You've thought about the old land and the new land—as well as some things you can start cleaning up to pave the way to the new land.

You've thought about your runway.

Have I convinced you yet that this is not time to throw in the towel on your life? That it's not the time to coast through the remaining decades? Rather, it's time to lean into a new vision for what your future holds for you.

In my first book, *Women Who Spark,* I introduced the concept of operations and special projects. The operations part of your life represents the things you do every day to keep things afloat and to address the multiple areas of your life. A few examples include taking care of your health and fitness, organizing your home and space, deepening your friendships, and finding time for your spiritual well-being.

Special projects represent the big things you may choose to go after. They allow you to pursue passion projects or uncover a bigger purpose. While you are tending to the effectiveness of your life's operations, you may also think more seriously about your broader contribution to others. What is your purpose in life? What are you here on this earth to do? Who are you meant to impact? Whose life can you affect in positive ways? Who inspires you? What has been whispering to you?

As I think about bridges and runways, I process it like this: I am always striving to "uplevel" the areas of my life that represent the operations side of things. I might think about this as crossing the bridge to the new land. In the new land, I reignite things. I get my health back under control, I declutter my house so I can feel more peaceful, I start to spend more time with my spouse, or I take a class to position myself for a promotion at work.

If I'm thinking about reinvention—you know the big stuff—I'm heading straight to the airport, getting on a plane, and speeding down the runway for take-off.

I've done a lot of bridge crossing, especially as I made the transition into my post-child-raising years. I discovered hobbies, decluttered my house, got serious about friendships, and started to eat less sugar.

And, I got on the plane for sure! In 2018, I wrote my first book, started the *Women Who Spark* brand, and am now dedicated to a mission of helping hundreds of thousands of women find greater happiness, confidence and sense of purpose in their lives during my next two decades.

Do you have bridges and runways in your future?

If you are approaching your 50s—or have already passed that milestone—you've experienced a lot in your life. It's likely all of your dreams did *not* come true. Or maybe you never dreamed big enough in the first place. You've experienced some disappointments in life, possibly a lot of them. Your difficult experiences may have been extremely painful and the trauma of deep loss may be a constant presence in your life.

Maybe your life hasn't been sprinkled with difficulties as such, but you're ready for more. You want to make changes in order to live a more fulfilling, meaningful, and robust life. It's possible you've settled for comfortable and good enough. Is a desire for more excitement gnawing at you?

Do you have an underlying restlessness that you can't put your finger on? If you do, you're not crazy. And you are not alone.

A number of years ago, a friend of mine visited from out of state. My husband and I took her and three of our kids out for dinner. Always the goofball, my husband had everyone laughing and bantering. We also had a great time during the process of ordering wine and, my husband's favorite, bourbon. Later, when we were back home and chatting, my friend said to me, "You are so lucky." I asked what she meant, and she said, "You have so much fun as a family. We don't have fun. Everyone is so serious. I feel very bored with my life."

I felt bad for her. From the outside looking in, her life looks perfectly wonderful. Only she knows what is smoldering deep within her heart.

Is there something inside your heart that you need to be working on? You simply have too much time left to coast. We are biologically designed to start a new life in our 50s. Menopause tells us it's time to be independent again. Our child-bearing years are over. Your kids, if you have them, are likely around for only a few more years—or already gone—and you may be ready for a new career challenge. What about hobbies, interests, passions, and other unrealized dreams?

**It's time to discover your best life right now.**

As you reflect on your life—both past and future—you'll likely recognize that it's marked by one or two-decade increments. For example, most childhoods last from about age 0 to age 20; launching into adult life, ages 20 – 30; child raising and career building from 30 – 50. But then what happens? I know many women in their 50s who are restless for change. They may not have consciously connected with the idea of change, but they've definitely connected with the idea that they are grappling with disappointment of some kind, that they've somehow given up who they are to take care of the needs of everyone around them

Age 50, give or take a number of years, marks our transition into our later years.

Making that transition successfully and thriving in your later years is what this book is all about. Remember, this is a new beginning. The second half of your life has an incredible amount of potential.

Look at the chart below. I love it. I came across this in a book called *Don't Retire, Rewire.*[3]

| | |
|---|---|
| Ages 45 – 64 | Middle Life |
| Ages 65 – 74 | Young Old |
| Ages 75 – 84 | Middle Old |
| Ages 85 – 95 | Old Old |
| Ages 95+ | Frail |

Some women may take exception to this framework, but I am confident it nets out the buckets of the second half of our life nicely.

Do you want to squander this precious second half of life? How many women in their 40s already feel old? They don't realize how much time they have.

How do you think about your life? You might look at it this way:

If you have 40 more years of life left, that is 14,600 days and 350,400 hours.

If you have 50 years left, that is 18,250 days and 438,000 hours.

This is a lot of time. What will you do with it?

## A Glance at Your Decades

Before we go further, I want you to consider what your past decades looked like. After all, they brought you to where you stand now. Most importantly, those past decades contributed to your current mindset.

As you read through these lists, think about your own experiences. Check the items on the list that come closest to representing each phase of your life.

This memory-refreshing exercise may provide insights into your current land, as well as your readiness to step on the bridge or head straight to the airport to hop a plane and hit the runway!

**From 0 – 18 years (childhood):**

- ☐ Did you grow up a fairly traditional dependent?
- ☐ Was there a strong sense of family culture and leadership from your parents?
- ☐ Did you receive structured learning in an educational system or at home with your parents?
- ☐ Do you look back on these years fondly?
- ☐ Were they difficult years?
- ☐ Did you rely almost entirely on your parents for financial support, at least until your teen years?
- ☐ Or did you support yourself in large part?
- ☐ Did your parents' encouragement foster a belief that you can go after your dreams? That you can do and be whatever you want?
- ☐ Or did your parents steer you toward their dreams for you?

- ☐ Did high school feel like the best years of your life?
- ☐ Or was high school a difficult experience for you? (One you're glad to have behind you!)

**Reflections:** What was great about these decades? What was a struggle? What was missing?

______________________________________________

______________________________________________

______________________________________________

______________________________________________

**From 18 – 30 years (transition into adulthood):**

- ☐ Did you attend college or a technical school?
- ☐ Did you begin your working profession at some point during this decade?
- ☐ Did you, like many young adults, meet your "person"?
- ☐ Did you get married during this decade?
- ☐ Did you buy your first house?
- ☐ Did you give birth to or adopt children?
- ☐ Did you struggle with the inability to have children?
- ☐ Did you begin thinking about your goals for your life? If you're a high achiever, did you even write them down?
- ☐ Did you feel excited?
- ☐ Did you feel like you had your whole life ahead of you?
- ☐ Did you have an idealistic view of a happy, joyful life ahead of you?

- ☐ Did you drift happily through this decade?
- ☐ Did your mess start early?

**Reflections:** What was great about these decades? What was a struggle? What was missing?

______________________________________________

______________________________________________

______________________________________________

______________________________________________

**From 30 – 50 years (early stage):**
These years mark what I like to refer to as the "messy middle" of life. The messy middle starts out manageable, most commonly marked by a sense of a lot going on.

- ☐ Did you earn an advanced degree or a different degree?
- ☐ Did you begin settling into a new marriage?
- ☐ Did you give birth to or adopt children?
- ☐ Did you begin juggling your work with the kids and taking care of your home?
- ☐ Did you spend a few years sorting through some of the challenges of marriage that you didn't anticipate? (This could have ranged from minor annoyances to more egregious problems.)
- ☐ Did you focus on achieving the goals you identified in your 20s? (At least the ones that still remained on your list.)
- ☐ Did you experience financial pressures as life became more multi-faceted, with more things vying for your dollars? (This might have included

daycare, kids' clothes, supplies and activities, saving for college for multiple kids, saving for retirement, paying the mortgage, facing the challenges of becoming a one-income family, paying an endless number of bills each month, and falling in the trap of credit card debt accumulation.)

- ☐ Did you trade in your young-adult car for a family mini-van?
- ☐ Did your schedule fill up with meal planning, shopping, cooking, carpools, volunteering at school, fitting in workouts, making sure your parents have what they need, laundry, cleaning, planning playdates and birthday parties, finding date nights, and keeping a social calendar active?
- ☐ Did your time with friends become a distant memory?
- ☐ Did you start struggling to fit in workouts?
- ☐ Did you begin feeling overwhelmed and exhausted?
- ☐ Did you still believe you could have it all? You wanted it, after all, so why wouldn't it happen?

**Reflections:** What was great about these decades? What was a struggle? What was missing?

________________________________________

________________________________________

________________________________________

________________________________________

**From 30 – 50 years (late stage):**
You're not seeing double. This is the same age range as above. A lot happens during these messy middle years, so I'm breaking it down by early and late stages. As these years go by, you may find things becoming more difficult than you intended.

- ☐ Things have remained harried, hurried, and messy.
- ☐ You spent so many years taking care of the needs of others that your needs got left behind.
- ☐ Somewhere along the way, you lost your own voice.
- ☐ Many days it feels like your family doesn't appreciate what you do for them.
- ☐ Professionally, your career didn't progress the way you thought it would.
- ☐ You lost your passion for your career.
- ☐ You lost your confidence over the years.
- ☐ You deal with regrets for the things you did or the things you didn't do.
- ☐ Your dreams are unfulfilled.
- ☐ You often feel lonely, even though you're surrounded by people.
- ☐ You vacillate between feeling happy and feeling sad.
- ☐ You're disappointed with a number of things in your life.
- ☐ You feel self-conscious because of your weight and find yourself declining invitations because of it.
- ☐ You're feeling stuck in a difficult marriage or relationship.
- ☐ You're feeling restless.

**Reflections:** What was great about these decades? What was a struggle? What was missing?

________________________________________

________________________________________

________________________________________

________________________________________

________________________________________

**What are your insights from this activity?**

What did you learn by reflecting on your experiences throughout the decades?

________________________________________

________________________________________

________________________________________

________________________________________

________________________________________

What surprised you?

________________________________________

________________________________________

________________________________________

________________________________________

________________________________________

In what ways have your experiences affected your current state of mind or your current level of readiness to step onto the bridge?

________________________________________

________________________________________

________________________________________

________________________________________

________________________________________

## Your Fork in the Road: Reinvent, Reignite, or Settle

So here you are. Somewhere in the messy middle of life or figuring out how to move on to the next phase. Only you know the degree to which you are struggling.

The big question, as you move toward your future decades—the second half of your adult life—is what will you do?

- ☐ Will you settle?
- ☐ Will you reignite your purpose?
- ☐ Will you reinvent your life?

Before we delve into the meaning of these three options, rest assured, the first half of life does not have to predict what will happen during your second half. In fact, it doesn't matter if the first half of your life was a D.I.S.A.S.T.E.R.! You can create a fresh start for yourself.

It starts with the decision to do it.

I'm inspired by the words of Robert Frost in his poem, *The Road Not Taken:*

*Two roads diverged in a yellow wood,*
*And sorry I could not travel both*
*And be one traveler, long I stood*
*And looked down one as far as I could*
*To where it bent in the undergrowth;*

*Then took the other, as just as fair,*
*And having perhaps the better claim,*
*Because it was grassy and wanted wear;*
*Though as for that the passing there*
*Had worn them really about the same,*

*And both that morning equally lay*
*In leaves no step had trodden black.*
*Oh, I kept the first for another day!*
*Yet knowing how way leads on to way,*
*I doubted if I should ever come back.*

*I shall be telling this with a sigh*
*Somewhere ages and ages hence:*
*Two roads diverged in a wood, and I—*
*I took the one less traveled by,*
*And that has made all the difference.*[4]

This poem means so much to me. It contains a concept that changed my life for the better. While I had my seasons of fear, regret, and shame, I look back and know I was on a road less traveled than many of the women around me. This poem helped me see that.

**A lot of people think the worst that can happen to them is death. Actually, the worst thing that can happen is not living life in the first place.**

A lot of people think the worst that can happen to them is death. Actually, the worst thing that can happen is not living life in the first place. Sometimes when we overprotect ourselves and make a steady stream of safe decisions, we miss out on life itself.

Which road will you take? Will you choose to settle? Or will you take a path less traveled?

Perhaps you're not sure. Maybe you're asking, "What does it even mean to settle?"

Here is a list of things you might be thinking if you're settling:

- ☐ I don't have anything to offer.

- ☐ I'm not enough. My life has shown me that.
- ☐ I've lost my confidence and I doubt I will get it back.
- ☐ I've become invisible.
- ☐ I'll just fade away.
- ☐ I'm bored, depressed, angry, bitter, or regretful—and I don't have a clue what to do about it.
- ☐ I'm not like those other women.
- ☐ Why couldn't my life have turned out the way her's did?
- ☐ I guess this is it.
- ☐ I can make this be okay.

Do you see yourself in this list? If you do, how do you feel about settling in and riding out the hundreds of thousands of minutes you have left, accepting things as they are?

Or do you want to think about reigniting and reinventing?

I thought so.

## Reigniting and reinventing

Now, let's talk about the difference between these two concepts: reigniting and reinventing.

The differences might be a bit nuanced, but they are important. We'll look at reigniting as getting your spark back within the existing broad context of your life. And we'll view reinventing as a more significant transformation of ourselves involving more disruptive change.

Let's look at examples in the health area of your life:

- Reigniting may involve revamping your workout routine and incorporating something you've always been interested in doing but never got around to. You might add yoga, kickboxing, or rock climbing to your routine. Or perhaps, you'll train for your first half marathon. Your thought process may be, "I've got to do something different so I can fall in love with my workouts again." This realization makes it clear you need to reignite this part of your life and uplevel things.
- Reinventing may involve a transformation that is multi-faceted. You might realize you are on a dangerous trajectory as your weight increases, your diet remains laden with too many calories, and you consume too many empty calorie foods. You might also be on too many meds or you might have a chronic disease like diabetes becoming more serious. You might also spend way too much time on the couch watching TV. If so, it's time to create a new story for yourself.

Let's look at another example in the Home and Space area of your life.

- You may want to *reignite* your home and space by transitioning your home from earth tones to gray tones and remodel your kitchen with white subway tile, gray marbled countertops, and stainless steel appliances. You have a fresh new look.

- Or you may want to *reinvent* your home and space by selling your big five-bedroom stone colonial in an expensive area and moving to a small manageable condo in an urban area in a completely different part of the country.

Here's one more example in the career space:

- You may want to *reignite* your career by going back to school for an added certification or even an advanced degree, positioning yourself for a promotion within your current profession.
- Or you may want to *reinvent* your career by walking away from the big corporate job with great benefits to take a go at turning your lifelong hobby into a business or starting a non-profit.

## What does reigniting sound like?

- [ ] I can be healthier.
- [ ] I can get my home into better condition so I enjoy it more.
- [ ] I have an opportunity ahead of me, and I can go after it.
- [ ] I can get my act together and create financial security for myself.
- [ ] I can make a more conscious effort to develop friendships.
- [ ] I can do this.
- [ ] I can start volunteering when I retire.

- ☐ I can turn my son's room into my craft room when he leaves for college.
- ☐ I can start training for a half marathon now that I have the time.
- ☐ I can spend the coming year decluttering my house, so I feel more peaceful and relaxed.
- ☐ I can take up a new hobby that I've always been interested in.

## What does reinventing sound like?

- ☐ It's time for a whole new career.
- ☐ I'm going to go back to school for a degree in an entirely different field.
- ☐ It's time to regain my health by completely changing the food I buy and the way I eat. I'm trading in my sedentary lifestyle for an active one.
- ☐ I'm going to quit my corporate job, take a leap, and start my own business.
- ☐ I don't know exactly what I'm going to do, but I'm ready to significantly change myself and my life.

As you read this chapter what is coming to mind for you? What is resonating with you? What is your heart telling you to do?

Do you have a voice inside you telling you that you're being selfish? Your husband and kids need you. Your parents need you. Who are you to think you should be venturing off into some self-serving direction?

Stop.

This voice is not sharing facts with you. She is trying to trick you into thinking you are somehow not enough. You are.

How old are you? Assuming you live into your 80s, how many decades is that?

**Don't you deserve to live your life in a meaningful way? Do you have a purpose within you that has been knocking on the door to get out and jump into action?**

Don't you deserve to live your life in a meaningful way? Do you have a purpose within you that has been knocking on the door to get out and jump into action?

Remember what I said earlier. They—all of them—will be fine.

As you begin to move in the direction of your dreams, you can tell the people around you that you'll be there for them and—at the same time--you are ready to start revisiting some of the dreams that you stuffed way into the background years ago.

You might be surprised. Your kids may actually *want* to see you stepping up and taking responsibility for your own life, to fully live.

## Don't Manufacture Guilt for Others

One of the benefits of reigniting and reinventing your own life is that you won't pressure your kids—or anyone for that matter—to keep you happy and fulfilled. I know what that's like. I'm happiest when I'm with our kids, and I definitely feel moments of sadness when we don't *get* them because they're with their friends, other parents, or in-laws.

The last thing I'll do, though, is say or do anything to put pressure on them or make them feel guilty. I've heard moms whine. "Can't you at least spend a few hours with us?" "It's just that I was hoping you would be here." These kids have enough of a challenge to navigate the people who want to see them and who they want to see. In many situations, our married children have multiple sets of parents and grandparents, as well as friends who—in many cases—are as important to them as their families are.

I strongly encourage against putting a guilt trip on them. Part of your reigniting and reinventing is to create a life that is fulfilling for you, independent of what your kids are doing.

Are you ready to reignite and reinvent?

It's okay if you don't have a clue what that might be. For now, it's enough to know you're interested. The "how" will come in later chapters.

## Let's Get Real About the Tough Stuff

In 2010 Janet Black and her husband lost everything. Their home value had dropped over $100,000 in the crash of 2008, they were foreclosed on two years later, and in the blink of an eye, their net worth was gone. Janet cashed in her 401K and bought a motorhome.

She was 62 years old.

The struggles for Janet began a few years earlier, when in 2003, she was diagnosed with fibromyalgia. Slowly it became difficult for Janet to do her work as a nurse practitioner and, in 2010, she was forced to leave her profession and go on disability.

As time passed, she became depressed and overweight. Many things were not going well, including losing their health insurance. To help minimize the expense of meds for both herself and her husband, Janet began to learn more about alternative medicine and supplements.

During this time, Janet's husband attended a conference where a speaker talked about *The Miracle Morning*, by Hal Elrod. He told Janet about the book, and it changed her life. Janet put a number of the teachings into practice: she began meditation, exercise, journaling, reading, and goal setting.

Those life changes set a number of things in motion, leading Janet to come off all of her medications, reverse her diabetes, and lose weight.

During this process, she was also reminded that she had written a book that she had never shared with the world. She dug out the manuscript and self-published her first book in 2014 at age 66. Today Janet is 72 years old. She has written and published eight books and is currently writing her ninth to chronicle her journey as a cancer patient.

She and her husband own a home again, they are building financial stability, and Janet said she is happier than she has ever been.

Her advice: No matter how hard it gets, things will change. You can help change things. Focus on "what it is that you want, set goals, and work toward that."

## Chapter Highlights

**Chapter 1: Is There More to Life Than This?**

- Get clear about what is nagging at you, feels unresolved, and needs your attention.

**Chapter 2: Let's Get a Few Things Straight**

- You have a runway ahead of you for the second half of your life and can change your beliefs about what lies ahead.

**Chapter 3: The Sparks Have Dimmed**

- Many mid-life women experience apathy. You can treasure the memories in your positive bucket and do the work to leave the negative bucket of memories behind.

**Chapter 4: Clean Up the Things That Matter to You**

- When you look around, what do you notice? As you assess ten areas of your life, what areas need to be cleaned up? Which need to be reignited and reinvented?

**Chapter 5: Women Who Took Action to Clean Up the Mess**

- A bridge connects the old land to the new land. You don't have to have a clear picture of your new land to step onto the bridge.

**Chapter 6: It's Time to Reignite and Reinvent**

- You may very well have three, four, or five decades left.
- You have a choice to make: settle where you're at, reignite, or reinvent.
- Reigniting involves getting your spark back within the existing broad context of your life.
- Reinventing is a more significant transformation—a more disruptive change.

# CHAPTER 7

## DESIGN YOUR 80-YEAR-OLD SELF

*It's important to grow old gracefully, and that's what I plan to do. I am here to stay. I take care of myself, and I have the discipline to stay fit and have good health until I am very old. I'm not planning on retiring, and in many ways, professionally at least, I think my best days are still to come.*

~ Sigourney Weaver

Have you ever thought about your 80-year-old self?

I have. In fact, this idea came to me by accident. I was speaking to a group of women a year ago, and disappointment was a life theme for many women in the audience. They had completed the "sadness, disappointment and struggle" checklist, and our debrief discussion left us all feeling like, "Well, shoot. I guess this is it. Life just didn't go the way we wanted it to. But maybe it's good enough."

I started thinking about my grandma, who was vibrant and amazing into her 80s. And I had an idea.

I said, "Ladies, I'm not an expert on guessing age, and it will be good for me to steer away from trying. As I look out into the audience, however, it looks like you have some decades left. Let's lean into your future. Imagine your 80-year old self. What is she doing? What does she look like? Who is she helping? What is she enjoying? What makes her laugh? What do her relationships look like? What are people saying about her? What legacy will she leave behind? Do you like her?"

I asked them to imagine their time between now and 80. "Do you have time to reignite and reinvent some things? Do you need to?"

Turns out, most of them had never looked at things that way. It instilled hope in them. This concept has not only shaped how I look at life—it's also had an impact on the people around me.

My friend, Susi, who will celebrate her 60th birthday in a few months, is one of them. My husband asked her if she is struggling with knowing this milestone birthday is coming up. She looked at me and said, "I'm not, because of you." Intrigued, of course, I wanted to know why.

Susi said, "I'm thinking about my 80-year old self, and she's going to be awesome. So, my 60th birthday doesn't bother me in the least. I'm ready to reinvent my life to have an amazing next two decades."

Sometimes inspiration can also come through envisioning a grim outcome you'd do almost anything to avoid. My sister, Sherri, credits her doctor's blunt warning with giving her back some extra decades. She made it clear Sherri had to get her health and weight under control—or expect that her inaction would result in a disintegrating physical condition and even cut her life short.

**Sometimes inspiration can also come through envisioning a grim outcome you'd do almost anything to avoid.**

That got my sister's attention. She envisioned what would be happening over the next few decades if she didn't make some changes. It was bleak enough to motivate Sherri to take some drastic measures to increase her chance of becoming a healthy 80-year-old woman: giving up sugar and increasing her exercise. Neither of those habits are easy to establish, but they are ways my sister is honoring and loving her future self.

I want you to stop for a moment and think about a woman you know who is in her 80s or 90s, still living a vibrant life.

Pause.

Yes, I really want you to think of one.

...a lovely, vibrant, still-living-life older woman *you* know.

**Your Inspiring Woman**

- Who is she?
- What is she doing?
- What does she look like?
- Who is she helping?
- What is she enjoying?
- What makes her laugh?
- What do her relationships look like?
- What are people saying about her?
- What legacy is she leaving behind?

Because of how we operate in society, a lot of attention is given to age 65. But I don't want you to shortchange yourself. There's a lot of life to be lived in the next few decades. To put the time you have left in perspective, let's look at what you've accomplished in life up to this point.

In 20 years, you grew from being a newborn to an adult. If you raised children, 20 to 30 years was enough time to raise an entire family into adulthood. You may also have navigated through several stages of a meaningful career in that same amount of time. You now face an opportunity to grow as much in 20 years in the future as you did in the past.

Let's not stop at 65! I'd like you to envision your 80-year old self. What is she doing?

Twenty years is a *long* time. Let's not waste them.

What about you? Have you given yourself enough runway in your future to be on fire, to wake up every day eager to leap out of bed, to make a difference for people around you, to leave a legacy behind, to have hope?

Some things to consider as you ponder your 80-year old self:

1. **How are you interacting with your friends and family?**

   Have you made decisions about your positive, active participation in the life of your family? Are you a joyful, helpful, non-imposing mother and grandma? Have you decided to be proactive in fostering healthy, enjoyable, engaging friendships with other women?

2. **What is your level of fitness and health?**

   Oh boy. This is a big one. A year ago, a friend told me, "Over time, my fitness has decreased, and my weight has increased. I need to do something about this." After coming to that realization, she went to work and a year later she's fit and lighter.

What does your eighty-year-old self look like? And what does your current self need to be doing to start growing into her. If you're more sedentary than you want to be, can you increase your level of activity and make it a part of your life? If you eat too much sugar, can you become a person who doesn't eat sugar? If you drink too much wine, can you start to limit yourself to one glass?

3. **How are you generating income?**

This is one of your greatest mind-shift opportunities. For all of the fear women have about their financial security, you have to remember that your income-producing capability does not end at age 65.

My lovely grandmother generated income until she was eighty as the organist at her church. She did not get paid an exorbitant amount of money, but she was paid enough to cover basic living expenses. Her home was paid for, she had money in the bank, and this stipend helped her not dip into her savings. My dad, who is 83, is also still generating income as a van driver for a local assisted living home. This follows a long career in the construction industry. Continuing to be productive and paid in your later years is a fantastic option to consider.

4. **How are you making a difference in the world?**

George Bernard Shaw put it this way,

> This is the true joy in life, the being used for a purpose recognized by yourself as a mighty one; the being thoroughly worn out before you are thrown on the scrap heap; the being a force of Nature instead of a feverish selfish little clod of ailments and grievances complaining that the world will not devote itself to making you happy.
>
> I am of the opinion that my life belongs to the community, and as long as I live, it is my privilege to do for it whatever I can. I want to be thoroughly used up when I die, for the harder I work, the more I live. Life is no 'brief candle' to me. It is a sort of splendid torch which I have got hold of for a moment, and I want to make it burn as brightly as possible before handing it on to the future generations.

I have nothing to add here. I love this.

5. **How are you impacting lives?**

   Wherever you're at in your life, you still have time to do the work necessary to leave a legacy behind. You can change the world by affecting the life of just one person. I bet you'll keep going and make numerous lives better because you were here.

## A Deeper Look at Your Vision

In order to truly grasp this concept, we need to take a methodical approach. After all, how you see your future self will be instrumental in how you take action.

Below are five scenarios for what your life may look like as you move through the next two or three decades.

As you read through each scenario, you may want to envision the season of your life beyond actively raising your children (if you have them) and actively working in your lifelong profession. In other words, these scenarios can help paint the picture for what could be next for you. Which scenario best summarizes how you see yourself living your second half of life?

**Scenario #1:** You are living a quiet, peaceful life. You spend time with your spouse or significant other, as well as your adult kids, grandkids, and friends. You enjoy cooking and baking, you help with your grandchildren, you get together with your girlfriends to golf or play bridge, and you enjoy time to relax during your day.

**Scenario #2:** You have moved beyond your lifelong career or your years as a stay-at-home mom, and continue to actively work in a job (maybe different than what you've done in the past) or volunteer activity. You want to live a life in which you contribute to an organization or to a community. You like being busy and waking up every day with somewhere to go. You like a full and busy calendar.

**Scenario #3:** You are living a life of adventure. You are traveling the world, or you've taken up an extreme hobby that you feel passionate about. You dedicate hours to this passion. It might be rock climbing, iron man competitions, competitive body building, surfing, or hiking.

**Scenario #4:** You have decided to run a non-profit. You've become an executive director of an existing non-profit, or you've started a non-profit of your own. Or maybe you've started your own business. Perhaps you've even turned a hobby into a business, or you've researched and identified a franchise opportunity to invest in. It's possible you've left your corporate job and started a consulting business doing the kind of work you've spent decades perfecting.

**Scenario #5:** This scenario is special. You can pair it with any of the above options. You have reinvented the brand of you. This scenario will be most likely used if you have neglected yourself over the years. Now, it's time to be excited about *you.* This might involve any number of things. You may choose to become healthier. This may include food choices, exercise, and your hair, make-up and wardrobe. Perhaps you've spent so much time taking care of everyone else that you've neglected doing things that will help you feel good about yourself. Is it time for a new you? Or perhaps you have been an unhappy, complaining, critical, gossipy kind of woman over the years. Is it time to become more friendly, cheerful, positive and forgiving? (Even—or especially—toward yourself?)

Which of the above scenarios resonate with you? There is no right answer. You get to decide. The important thing is that you are thinking about this. Your future vision will influence—or should influence—your present-day habits and choices.

**Your future vision will influence—or should influence—your present-day habits and choices.**

## Your Vision of You

It's time to create the vision for your future.

**Your 80-Year-Old Self.**

- Who is she?
- What is she doing?
- What does she look like?
- Who is she helping?
- What is she enjoying?
- What makes her laugh?
- What do her relationships look like?
- What are people saying about her?
- What legacy is she leaving behind?

## How Do You Feel About Your Vision?

Last year I created a vision board of my 80-year old self. I have it in my office. It reminds me:

- As of right now—I have 23 more years before I am 80.
- I want to be a cheerful, kind, helpful 80-year old woman. I found a photo of a woman who looks like this—to remind me—and put her on the board.
- I want to be in good health and living a fit lifestyle.

Knowing these things influences not only my do's and don'ts for any given day, but it also inspires me to take on more—because I have time.

I encourage you to take time to create your own vision board.

Would you like some inspiration?

Visit www.womenwhosparkbooks.com. In the resources section, you will find a process for how to create your vision board.

## What Do Other Women Envision?

The three women below shared their visions of their 80-year-old selves. Currently, they are in their 50s and 60s (you will read about their life reinventions in Chapter 12).

**Cathy Studer**, age 54, sees herself as a compassionate grandmother who has a sweet smile and love for life.

She lives in a small condo close to her children and grandchildren. Cathy loves starting her day with a cup of coffee and the Today Show. During the rest of her day, she enjoys reading books, spending time with her grandchildren, and vacationing near the ocean.

What brings Cathy more joy than anything else is listening to people in her home laugh and smile. Her relationships are meaningful and a priority to her.

People who know Cathy will say that she is a sweet soul who has empathy and compassion for everyone's story. She has been a warrior in defeating childhood sexual abuse. As a speaker and coach, she has guided numerous people into healing and wholeness leading to their betterment.

Cathy will leave a legacy of being part of a movement to eradicate the childhood sexual abuse statistics. Through her book, *Broken to Beautifully Whole*, hundreds of thousands of people have stepped into becoming Kintsugi and healing their own hurts, traumas, or brokenness. Cathy has left her family knowing the importance of creating positive experiences and memories over collecting things.

**Mandy Hinerman**, age 64, sees her 80-year old self as a strong, healthy, confident women who inspires others to find their own creativity and passions.

She is creating, whether it's art, pastries, food—anything that brings joy to herself and others. She sees herself volunteering at a neighborhood school, her church, and in the community. She's there for whoever needs help: family, friends, neighbors, and other community members.

She is enjoying her life! She sees herself spending time outdoors and playing tennis—perhaps even better than she played a few decades earlier. She laughs easily, inspired by her husband, children, grandchildren, and her pets.

She is known by the people around her as a fulfilled, honest, and intentional woman. Best of all, they will be heard saying, "I want to be like her when I'm 80."

Mandy wants to be remembered as a light—a woman who loved others well and used her God-given gifts and talents to brighten other peoples' lives.

**Terry Fulcher, age 64,** describes her 80-year-old self as bright and curious about all things! She is active in her church, her community and in the lives of her family members.

She continues to attend church—both large services and small groups—and loves to listen to the women of all ages around her. She volunteers her organizational skills to women's activities as needed and is the oldest woman in her book club. She enjoys books, likely audible or large print by now. She may even lead an online book club.

She teaches at the local college and supports the Leadership & Innovation Department in any way she can. When not actively teaching, she is a mentor to students and younger faculty as they learn and grow in their leadership skills. She is helping college students study, learn, and edit their papers.

She continues to help her children, grandchildren, and great-grandchildren enjoy time together. She provides advice when asked and support when needed. She envisions herself laughing with her family. Her great-grandchildren will regularly tell their parents, "Let's go to Mema's house! I want to see her!"

Terry's family will be available to help her with physical projects—cleaning the gutters, mowing the lawn, plowing the snow, scrubbing the baseboards, and washing the carpets. They will be in and out of her house sharing chats and having meals together. They will pick her up for holidays or they will still all be coming to her house.

Her church friends will continue to come together to laugh and enjoy conversations. She may still be the one organizing outings.

People will tell her, "There is NO WAY you are 80! I can't believe it"

They will tell others, "Ask Terry—she will help you figure out what to do! She is amazing at that!"

Terry envisions she has left behind the changes she initiated during her professional life—they are hard-wired into the work people do now. They may not know they were *her* ideas. But it's her legacy all the same. She created the expectation of professionalism on every team she led. She worked hard with dedication and passion to make everything better.

Her family remembers her for her generous and caring heart—how she gave support and stood with them through good and difficult times. Her family continues to have a love for music. Many of them sing, dance, or play because music has always been a part of their lives.

## Let's Get Real About the Tough Stuff

I've only known Carol as an 80-year old lovely, sparkly, kind woman. I met her through a friend of mine who had officially adopted Carol to be her mom.

I was immediately drawn to her kind, friendly nature. "I'm not that worldly," Carol told me, "but I love people."

Carol and her husband, Shorty, enjoy busy social lives.

> We're having fun at this stage of our life, going out, as well as entertaining people in our home. It helps to have a husband who is always out and about. I don't know many people at 80 who still do as many things as we do. We can still drive. So many can't. We have friends whose health changed in an instant. We're grateful for our good life. We've had sadness, we've had happiness. It's not perfect, but we're very happy.

Carol and I talked more, and she told me about the interests she and Shorty have shared together over the years. Perhaps most notably, they have been avid football fans, holding tickets for both University of Wisconsin football and the Green Bay Packers. Those years created a lot of fun for Carol and Shorty.

She also reflected on her years as a hairdresser. Carol loved her work and learned to navigate some of the challenges of working with up to a dozen women. Carol said, "When there are clashes, you just have to step back and let some things go."

I recall thinking, "*What a charmed life,*" as Carol summarized her life with these reflections:

> You kind of flow from one age to the next. I feel that I've been spoiled. I had my own little business and I had the support from my husband. Our parents were generous along the way, as well, and we were given things. We've worked very hard. I have a great husband, and I've had a great life.

I've learned, as you know, that most women experience a messy middle on their life journey, even a desert to cross.

I asked Carol, "What about hard times?"

"Our son, John, was our messy middle." Carol told me. "Because of our son's bi-polar, our life was often difficult, and I felt sad much of the time. I remember feeling, 'I wish I could just be worry-free.'" Her son passed away in 2015, making his own choice not to continue his life. He was 57 years old.

Carol said, "I don't even want to know the things I don't know. During my working years, I would get phone calls during the day, very scary things going on, prompting 911 calls. We tried for years to get answers, but John often felt he knew more than his psychiatrists. He could not humble himself to listen. All of these things were very difficult. I hardly slept many of those years." I asked Carol how many of her middle years were really difficult? She answered, "Many decades."

Today, Carol is one of the most gracious women I have met. She is in a happy stage of life, and every time I see her, I know without question I want to be just like her 23 years from now.

**Chapter Highlights**

**Chapter 1: Is There More to Life Than This?**

- Get clear about what is nagging at you, feels unresolved, and needs your attention.

**Chapter 2: Let's Get a Few Things Straight**

- You have a runway ahead of you for the second half of your life and can change your beliefs about what lies ahead.

**Chapter 3: The Sparks Have Dimmed**

- Many mid-life women experience apathy. You can treasure the memories in your positive bucket and do the work to leave the negative bucket of memories behind.

**Chapter 4: Clean Up the Things That Matter to You**

- When you look around, what do you notice? As you assess ten areas of your life, what areas need to be cleaned up? Which need to be reignited and reinvented?

**Chapter 5: Women Who Took Action to Clean Up the Mess**

- A bridge connects the old land to the new land. You don't have to have a clear picture of your new land to step onto the bridge.

**Chapter 6: It's Time to Reignite and Reinvent**

- You may very well have three, four, or five decades left, and you have a choice to settle for where you're at, reignite, or reinvent.

**Chapter 7: Design Your 80-Year Old Self**

- Envision a lovely woman you know who is in her 80s.
- Think about your own 80-year-old self.
- Determine which scenario most resonates with you for this stage of your life.
- Create a vision board.

# CHAPTER 8

## Inspiration From Women in Their 70s, 80s And 90s

*I look forward to being older, when what you look like becomes less an issue and what you are is the point.*

~ Susan Sarandon

Recently, I was booked to speak for a women's club in my community. As we chatted about thc ideas behind living a life that sparks, the president of the club said, "Some of these women are still living life, and others not so much. You'll want to make sure your comments are relevant to the audience."

I was intrigued by the idea. These women were attending events. Yet, aside from the once-a-month opportunity to drag themselves out of the house for the women's luncheon, they remained holed up in their homes, possibly with the blinds drawn.

I believe that attitude is a choice.

I do realize that many women experience setbacks that are out of their control. Health and mobility issues may create an unwanted situation where the mind may be willing but the body unable. But we can do everything possible to ensure we embrace life to the best of our abilities.

I love seeing women who are on fire into their later years.

In this chapter, you'll meet a few women living their lives fully into their 70s, 80s, and 90s.

## My Grandma

I hear the words of my grandma echoing in my mind almost every day. *"Honey, they're doing the best they can."*

Bertha Mae, my lovely grandma, was one of the kindest women I have ever known. She saw the best in everyone, right up until the day she died at age 89. She never had a cross word to share.

I am inspired by her to be a productive, contributing member of my family and community until … well, forever.

As I think about my 80-year old self, I think about her. I want to be like her. She lived a full life. Her calendar was robust as she managed her many responsibilities and interests.

After operating a small department store, along with my grandpa, in her small town of Brodhead,

Wisconsin—population 3000—for decades, she continued serving her community as an alderwoman for two terms. And for as long as I can remember, she served as the organist at her church. She picked up a few other odd jobs to keep busy and ensure her financial security.

My grandma always looked lovely and put together. She wore pretty clothes, had her hair done weekly, and applied the perfect amount of make-up. And she always—emphasis on *always*—had time to be an amazing grandma.

She taught me how to cook, bake, sew, knit, crochet, and do needlepoint. She had a profound impact on my life, especially after my mom left our family. My grandma was always available to us when we needed her—and she was always welcoming and generous.

It wasn't until her early 80s that she had to slow down as she gradually lost her eyesight. Her final few years were difficult for her, but she remained lovely and cheerful until the end of her life.

## Suzanne Bander, Age 96

Suzanne Bander is an amazing grandma and great grandma, according to her daughter, Mandy Hinerman.

Even as her eyesight has been failing her over the past few years, Suzanne still never misses a birthday or anniversary within her family of several children, grandchildren, and great grandchildren. She's been mailing cards and notes for decades.

Suzanne keeps track of all of the names, dates and addresses in an address book she has been carrying since the 1960s. As new members come into the family through marriage or birth, she's quick to update her book. Recently, Mandy's sister moved to a new home.

Their mom said, "Be sure to send me her new address. I want to send them a card to congratulate them on their new home."

All of Suzanne's grandchildren, though they live in different states, feel connected with her because of her consistent correspondence and acknowledgment over the years.

Up until the past two years, Suzanne kept very active, attending women's events, playing cards several times a week and attending her stretching classes. She, along with her 91-year-old husband, lives independently. Though she no longer drives, her husband does.

Suzanne worked into her 80s and was always put together. Mandy said she got her hair done weekly, always wore make-up, and paid attention to her wardrobe. She's been happy in her later years.

And yes, there was a messy middle. Mandy's dad died when he was 50 years old. Mandy told me that it wasn't until recently that she understood just how difficult this time had been for her mom, becoming a widow at such an early age. She and her husband had shared an active social life, and that dried up after he passed away.

Three years later, Suzanne was married to a man with a large, active, vivacious family. She blossomed during that season of her life and remains happily married 42 years later.

While life is good, Suzanne has some regret. She told Mandy during a recent interview session, "I wish I had gotten a formal education. In my later years, so many of the women I've interacted during my later years are retired teachers. It reminds me that I wish I had gone to college."

## Donna, Age 85

I met Donna when one of my friends told me, "I know someone you have to talk to. She is truly a delight. Her smile is infectious, her attitude is always positive, and her perspective of the world is one of compassion." Now that I've met her—I agree! Donna is the perfect example of a woman who sparks well into her 80s, even when life throws a few curve balls.

Donna is currently in the midst of her third battle against cancer, and you would only know it if someone told you.

Donna credits her happy, positive nature to her upbringing. She shared,

> My mom did not let me feel sorry for myself. Ever. Whatever was happening for me, she consistently shared, 'I know this is hard for you, but there are so many people who have a more difficult situation than you.' My mom combined her love and care for me with a reminder that I didn't need to go through my life feeling sorry for myself. She wanted me to feel confident but also empathetic to others around me.

She continued,

> I've always tried to be happy. I loved life. But that doesn't mean it wasn't hard, because it was. And that doesn't mean I was always happy, because I wasn't. My husband traveled a lot, and I dealt with the kids. My husband died 15 years ago, and I was devastated. I even had to switch my church so I wasn't reminded of him every time I walked in.

> Today I have four granddaughters, a grandson and a great granddaughter. I am very happy.

Donna told me, "I don't think young people today will want to hear what I have to say. My message is about priorities. We should all put God, our family, and our country first. Not everyone wants to hear this."

I told Donna I believe that is exactly what we need.

## Nancy Briggs, 79

The last thing Nancy said to me the day I talked to her is "It's never over. It will never be over."

Her story is lovely. And she is living her life fully alive today.

A year and a half ago, after believing her entire life that her father had died during WWII before she was born, she discovered that her dad had, in fact, returned from the war. During conversations with four cousins she found on Ancestory.com, she learned her father was among a group of 80 men who bombed Tokyo at the beginning of WWII, called the Doolittle Raiders. They crashed in China and 77 survived. Her father was rescued, came back, married, and had six children.

Nancy also discovered she has six half brothers and sisters she had not known about her entire life, and they did not know about her—until that moment. They had lived in the same state all of her life. So close and yet so far away. Meeting them was the most fearful and fulfilling time of her life.

> I am now connected with them. The last year and a half, I've been very busy with these new siblings who have embraced me fully. This has been a huge

change in my life, going from an only child to being the oldest of seven siblings.

Thinking about her life now, Nancy said:

Nothing has really changed—well, beyond six newly discovered brothers and sisters— in my life of aging except the way I walk and the way I move, much slower these days.

At this age, my heart has not changed, nor my mission in life. God is still teaching, and I am still learning to walk with Him daily.

Nancy is joyful today, but life hasn't always been joyful.

When she was in her late 20s, she went through an unwanted divorce, had a young child, and lost a two-day old baby. It was the most devastating time in her life. She had no one to turn to. During that time, she met her now-husband of 53 years and came to know God. Together, their lives were different from that point forward.

While Nancy worked as an elementary school teacher, she—at the same time—started speaking for Christian women's clubs, hosting retreats counseling women and teaching Bible Study Classes in her church. During those years, she and her husband moved 23 times, allowing Nancy to work with 100s of women from coast to coast. She remains in touch with many of those women, hearing from at least one of them almost every day.

In addition to the richness of the relationships of women she has ministered to for decades, she has two children, seven grandchildren, eight great grandchildren, six siblings, and her loving husband Gary of more than 50 years.

She wrote a book about 20 years ago for her grandchildren to help them understand about life. The book centered on her relationship with God as her Father, because there wasn't a father in her life. When she was born, they skipped over the line on the birth certificate for who the father was. Because Father God said HE would be her Father, each time she read the book to her grandchildren, she would weep. He is still a Father to the fatherless.

Nancy's life testimony had been built around this reality that God has been her Father since her birth. And now, she knows who her biological father was, and that he was alive for several decades, but who never knew her.

> Father God formed me from birth, but I wasn't introduced to him until my 20s. I parallel finding my earthly father the same as finding my Heavenly Father. I watched videos and news clips of him; I watched clips from the attack on Tokyo; I had a book he wrote a chapter in. I learned about him in letters. I went to see where he was buried and where his parents were buried. I became introduced to him through my brothers and sisters. It was the same way that I began to know Father God in His Word that I got to know my earthly father.

Nancy has a box where she's collected all of the things she has learned about this father. Finding about who he was has been a glorious experience for her. Nancy is excited to share stories about her father with her grandchildren and is feeling nudged to write another book.

Today, Nancy said, "Life is pretty simple; not boring but simple."

Every day is a new day, a different day. "If the phone rings and someone needs help, we help."

"I've never been a goal maker, but if I were, it would be for Father God to say to me, 'Well done my good and faithful Servant.'"

## Gloria Potter, 70

After retiring from a long career as an elementary school music teacher, Gloria was lonely during the day and missed the daily interactions with other teachers and students. She felt her life lacked purpose.

> I didn't have a place to connect with other people. When I retired three years ago, my group of friends had shrunk. What I needed to do at this point in my life was reach out and find a place where I could be needed and useful and have a group of new contacts and friends. I felt something was missing in my life.

Gloria has been a Christian her whole life, but for almost two decades, she could not find a church community that fulfilled her needs. She was also so busy that she didn't prioritize her faith needs.

Finally, that changed:

> At 69, I found St. Matt's in Wauwatosa and I have been so blessed. My pastors saw that I had gifts to use in service and encouraged me to use those gifts. That encouragement deepened my faith. I now live a spirit-filled life.

> I have made phone calls and written cards to the elderly and lonely. I have also been calling and writing letters to the EMT's and teachers—in the midst of the pandemic—to express our appreciation for their service.

Gloria sets a reminder on her phone at 9:00 am and 4:00 pm that says, "Reach out and share love and kindness." It only takes her a few seconds to send an email or text, or to stop and write a quick note. She has seen over and over how this small effort can brighten someone's day! She said, "I often get a text or phone call back saying, 'Wow you made my day! I really needed that! Your message came at the perfect time in my day/life!'"

"I am privileged through church connections and the ministry of outreach to call two women each week—one in her 80s and one in her 90s," Gloria said, "They are delightfully fun to talk with and have blessed my life with their humor, grace, and perspective."

Like almost every woman, Gloria's life was not without a messy middle. Her childhood was rough, with an emotionally unstable mom and a passive dad, and she experienced her own difficulties in her younger adult life. She and her husband lived through many years trying to conceive children, and Gloria also managed the challenges of being bipolar. Eventually, they were blessed with two beautiful adopted children, and Gloria's bipolar disorder has been well managed—with no symptoms—for 25 years. She said, "The reason I share these things is that yes, my life is blessed, but it's also how we look at life. We can take these challenges and let them beat us to the ground or give them to God. It takes trust and patience—and gratitude."

Gloria explained to me that the practice of gratefulness has strengthened her desire to reach out to others and share because she herself is so blessed.

> Being grateful when you step out of bed is where gratefulness starts. I suggest a blessing bowl where you write down your blessings and refer to them when you need a little nudge or are feeling a little down. Remembering your blessings is so up-lifting. It's then you feel compelled to reach out to others.

One of the church pastors had an idea to put devotionals on YouTube, and someone asked Gloria if she would be interested in doing one. She had to learn how to use the technology and feels glad God was able to find that ability within her. She said, "I create a video on my phone, move it to my computer, then forward the video, hymn and text by email to one of my Pastors." Not only did she do one, she has gone on to do several.

> My lessons in life taught me that we are capable of much more when encouraged by others and can serve when called upon. We all have gifts, but we must be encouraged and confident to use them. It brings joy and happiness and contentment to show compassion and bring joy to others. I feel fulfilled.
>
> I need to use this time that we have on earth to do more than read a book or watch the news. God is asking me to reach out. This has given my life purpose.

## Chapter Highlights

**Chapter 1: Is There More to Life Than This?**

- Get clear about what is nagging at you, feels unresolved, and needs your attention.

**Chapter 2: Let's Get a Few Things Straight**

- You have a runway ahead of you for the second half of your life and can change your beliefs about what lies ahead.

**Chapter 3: The Sparks Have Dimmed**

- Many mid-life women experience apathy. You can treasure the memories in your positive bucket and do the work to leave the negative bucket of memories behind.

**Chapter 4: Clean Up the Things That Matter to You**

- When you look around, what do you notice? As you assess ten areas of your life, what areas need to be cleaned up? Which need to be reignited and reinvented?

**Chapter 5: Women Who Took Action to Clean Up the Mess**

- A bridge connects the old land to the new land. You don't have to have a clear picture of your new land to step onto the bridge.

**Chapter 6: It's Time to Reignite and Reinvent**

- You may very well have three, four or five decades left, and you have a choice to settle for where you're at, reignite, or reinvent.

**Chapter 7: Design Your 80-Year Old Self**

- Envision a lovely woman you know who is in her 80s.
- Think about your own 80-year-old self.
- What scenario most resonates with you for this stage of your life?
- Create a vision board.

**Chapter 8: Inspiration From Women in Their 70s, 80s, and 90s**

- You can be fully alive in the later years of your life.

# PART IV

## FAN THE FLAMES

# CHAPTER 9

## BELIEVE IN YOURSELF

*If you hear a voice within you say "you cannot paint," then by all means paint, and that voice will be silenced.*

~ Vincent van Gogh

In 2017 I attended the Milwaukee Business Journal "Women of Influence" luncheon where Janette Braverman walked onto stage and accepted an award. There is no way to *not* be inspired by Janette.

She is the founder of Leaders Leaving Legacies, LLC and the author of *10 Reasons Communication Brings Transformation: Unleash Your Greatness.*[5] She is also the first African American to serve as a County Board

Supervisor of Ozaukee County, north of Milwaukee, WI, where I live.

She shared in her acceptance interview that she recently decided it is time for her to pursue her passions in her own life. One of those passions is to write. She said, "I decided last year I wanted to write a book, so I wrote a book."

Her timing was perfect. She gave me the inspiration I needed exactly when I needed it. I had decided 11 years earlier that I wanted to write a book, but I was doing a fantastic job of procrastinating. Women—you may already know—often procrastinate when they are uncertain. *What if I fail? What if I don't know what to do? How do I even start?*

That moment during that lunch with Janette on stage brought an end to my procrastination. I thought to myself, "She wrote a book in one year. If she can write a book, I believe I can write a book. I'm going to write my book next year." And I did.

I mentioned earlier in the book that you might find this sequence of thoughts helpful.

#1: Believe it's possible for someone.
#2: Believe it's possible for women like us.
#3: Believe it's possible for me.

According to a quick Google search, there are between 600,000 and 1,000,000 books published each year—depending upon which stats you believe. So, it's clearly possible. Next, all you have to do is visit Amazon to see the significant number of books written by women "like us."

So, yes, certainly, without any question, hesitation, or doubt, it is: 1) possible for someone, 2) possible for women like us—because Janette did it, and 3) possible for me—if I believe in myself.

Janette was one of the women on stage with the amazing bio winning the award. It's easy for the other 700 of us sitting at our table clapping to believe that we will never be like the 29 women winning the awards. Sometimes, though, the difference between us and them is that they're the ones taking action, pushing through fears and insecurities, figuring it out, taking their next best step on any given day, and even doing it afraid.

Janette later shared with me that she had been journaling for 10 years prior to writing her book. It was her transition into a pivotal time in her life—a time where she felt ready to pursue her passions—that led her to write her book.

It can be overwhelming if we get caught up with a whole series of questions: How did she do it? How is it even possible? How could I ever hold a book with my name on it? How does someone even write a book? How would I find a publisher?

Maybe you don't want to write a book, but I'll bet you've stood on the sidelines watching someone else achieve your dreams. What does it take to move from watching to doing? First of all, don't get tangled up trying to figure out the *how* right now.

Instead, get started with the *what* and have faith that the *how* will figure itself out. Here was my *what* at that moment: "I want to write a book." The first thing I had to do was believe in myself.

## Why Does Belief in Yourself Matter?

Belief precedes action. Without belief, you will stop short of trying. One of the biggest regrets women have at the end of their lives is that they didn't try. Without belief they don't try, and they die with their dreams still locked up inside of them.

If you believe in yourself, you will have more possibilities in your life. You will have more enthusiasm and more optimism. You will accomplish more. You will be on fire. You will be happier, more confident, and more purpose-driven. You will collapse into bed at night, exhilarated by what you did that day and eager to leap out of bed the next morning to get a new day started. Okay, maybe I'm pushing it on the "leap out of bed" part, but you know what I mean.

**If you believe in yourself, you will have more possibilities in your life.**

Amy recently described her life as "meh." She said, "I'm supporting my husband's dream, but I want to have my own dream. I don't know yet what it will be, but I know I want to have one."

Because Amy believes in herself, two things are happening: 1) She has confidence that she can discover what her dreams are, and 2) She believes she will be able to achieve them. She also, incidentally, has to believe that she *deserves* to have dreams of her own. I'm glad she does.

Ellen, mentioned earlier in the book, was struggling with anxiety and depression. At her husband's suggestion, she joined the Women Who Spark Boot Camp. She joined us, because she believed this would make a difference for her. It did. Ellen did the work, but the work never would have happened without the belief.

Belief is more important than confidence at this stage. While confidence is important, many women are confident in certain things but lack the belief they could do something better. If you don't believe in yourself, and in the outcome you want for yourself, so much gets left on the table.

- You don't pursue an ideal career.
- You don't ask for a raise.
- You don't invite a potential new friend for coffee.
- You don't start your own business.
- You don't stick to habits.
- You don't tackle a difficult project.
- You don't share your thoughts in meetings.
- You don't try something that looks complicated.
- You don't write the book that is inside of you.
- You don't sign up for the painting class.

This list is only the beginning.

Take a moment to think about what you're avoiding. Finish these two sentences:

One of the things I have always wanted to do but never felt confident enough to try is ______________ ________________________________________.

Because I've never tried this, I feel ____________ __________________________.

I've asked other women how they feel as a result of not trying. Here are some of the things they tell me:

- "I feel disappointed in myself."
- "I feel sad."

- "I feel like I'm not as good as the women around me."
- "I feel like I'm falling behind."
- "I feel like it's now too late."
- "I feel unfulfilled."
- "I feel bored."
- "I feel regretful."
- "I feel like I'm not a very good role model for my daughters."

Now, I want you to think of something you've tried—even though you felt unsure—and you were successful.

"I tried ________________________________________
______________________________."

"I felt ________________________________________
______________________________."

I've asked other women how they felt after they tried! Here is what they tell me:

- "I feel proud of myself.
- "I feel like I can figure anything out."
- "I feel fulfilled."
- "I feel happy."
- "I feel exhilarated."

Taking action and trying can go one of two ways: 1) try and succeed, or 2) try and fail.

I love both of these! They are both more courageous and more fulfilling than option three: never try.

A couple of years ago, my daughter, Steph—who was 27 years old—decided to make an apple pie with a lattice crust. She proudly took a photo of it and posted it on social media. I'd given up pie making years ago, having been taught many homemaking skills by my beautiful grandma. I sure never taught my daughters how to make a pie with a lattice crust.

I called Steph and asked, "What inspired you to make a pie?" She said, "I wanted to see if I could do it."

I love that story.

If you want to do something, even if you think you can't, try!

## Where Does Belief Come From?

The first step is recognizing our belief in ourselves is ultimately chosen. We often give others far too much power in influencing how we feel about ourselves. It doesn't have to be that way.

**We often give others far too much power in influencing how we feel about ourselves. It doesn't have to be that way.**

Your self-esteem, confidence, and belief in yourself are determined by you. You get to decide if the value you place upon yourself will be determined by words and action of others or by your internal belief in who you are as a person—a conviction that you are as worthy as the women around you.

It might not be easy, but you *can* rise up above the words spoken by others. It may help if you keep in mind that most people who speak negatively of others do so because of their own misery and feelings of inadequacy.

People who are strong, happy, and confident in who they are raise others up.

I was captivated recently by a public service announcement on television. In the opening scenes, the camera captured the thoughts of several young people. This is what they said:

- "Because of you, I felt hopeless."
- "Because of what you said about my work, I started to question my own voice."
- "Because of your negative comments online, I almost stopped doing the one thing that makes me happiest in life."

Then the message became more hopeful:

- "Because you said hi to me on the first day of school, I felt included, and I knew that I was going to be okay."
- "Because of you sharing your story with me, I felt comfortable sharing my own."
- "I'm still here today because of you."

It's wonderful when others help us feel good about ourselves, because then it's easy to believe in our value and in our capabilities. However, we also need to remember that someone has to make the first move to believe in themselves enough to not only achieve their dreams, but also inspire others. Are you willing to take that first brave step?

Are you willing to develop your own beliefs about yourself? Will you regain the power to control your feelings about your value and capabilities? Will you cultivate your own positive belief in yourself?

## Five Ways to Start Believing in Yourself:

Since we're talking about reigniting and reinventing your life, we'll talk about your belief in yourself in that context.

Whatever part of your life you want to reignite, you can!

If you want to reinvent your life, you can do that, too.

Start with these steps:

1. **Believe it's possible.**

The next time you look at another woman and think to yourself, *"I wish I could be like her,"* be sure to finish the thought with, *"Someday, I will be like her."*

When you are inspired by a new thought—regardless of what triggers the thought—and you have a momentary feeling of *"I wish I could________,"* shift your thinking to *"That is something I want to do."* Remember, the *how* can come later.

When I was 24 years old, I was participating in a sales training workshop. At that stage in my career, participating in corporate training was a new experience for me—and I loved it. During this particular session, the facilitator at the front of the room was capable, confident, and beautiful. She was wearing a beautiful red suit and high heels—black patent leather. I was mesmerized.

As I sat in that room, I was struck by a thought: *"I want to be her."*

I wanted to do what she was doing as a career, outfit and all. I had no idea how I would make that happen, but I knew it was what I wanted.

Through a sequence of events and conversations with people to gather information over the next three years, I eventually became my own version of her. I went back to school, got a master's degree in adult education and organizational science (a term I had never heard of before), and became a corporate trainer. After working as a sub-contract trainer for an international company for a few years, I started my own training company when I was 33 years old, along with my long-time business partner and friend, Nancy.

Twenty-five years later, our company is still providing training to companies all over the country. And, in case you're wondering, I did buy the red suit and black patent leather heels!

2. **Create a vision of what it looks like.**

The next step is to envision what your future will look like as you reignite or reinvent your life.

As you think ahead to your future vision, the picture you see will fall somewhere between a hazy concept of what you have in mind and a crystal clear picture of exactly what you will be doing. If you're more of a concrete thinker without much out-of-the-box creativity, this step may feel difficult for you. If you have a knack for creative thinking and a vivid imagination, you'll love this step.

Do you have absolutely no idea what your ideal future looks like? That's ok too. We're stepping through this together. You can think of this process as crossing the bridge to your new land. If the bridge is a long one, you may not be able to see the land. But you know it's there—and you know there is something there for you that will resemble the dream you have for yourself. I love the idea of gradually crossing the bridge and arriving at a new land that is even better than you imagined.

When my sister, Sherri, started to focus on her health—primarily giving up sugar and walking—she envisioned a healthier woman, one who would likely lose weight and one with a better emotional experience every morning as she got dressed for the day.

As she started to cross the bridge, one sugar-free day after the next, she got closer and closer to her new land—a land where she had reignited her health. What she didn't realize is that the new land held not only reignited health, it also included a reinvention of her 52-year-old self. During the process, she regained her athleticism. The strength and muscle tone of her youth has returned to her, and she has adopted a lifestyle of running 50 to 60 miles a week. She is now free of the chronic pain that was creeping into her life.

Sherri's story is a good example of how your visioning might work. She saw something worth working toward in the beginning, and what she found on the other side of the bridge was even better. I have a feeling she is only getting started. As she gets further and further into the new land, her life will continue to become even more beautiful because of her commitment to one thing: regaining her health and fitness.

Wherever you are, and whatever you see, right now is the perfect place to start.

Equipped with your vision, you can write about where you want to go in your journal, or you can create a vision board. Do whatever will help you put a stake in the ground. You can add to your vision as you learn more and as you begin to make progress.

3. **Think more about your past successes than about your past failures.**

As you think about your dreams to reignite or reinvent your life, where does your mind tend to take you?

If you've had a variety of ups and downs, successes and failures, and hits and misses over the years, you may be tempted to dwell on them. Your mind may quickly default to thinking, "Well, yeah but ..." Or you may think you can't experience future success because of past failures.

I encourage you to intentionally think about your ups, successes, and wins. Everyone's life is a blend of both. Every positive experience you've had is proof that you can succeed. Bring those thoughts along to encourage yourself along the way.

Also, remember, your past failures taught you something, each one of them. You are who you are because of them. Your future successes will come more easily because of what you've experienced in your past.

4. **Accept fear as a predictable part of your journey.**

Fear is a fact of life.

We are all afraid at one time or another.

When I wrote *Women Who Spark*, I had a gathering with a number of women who were helping film my book trailer. As the publication date neared, I felt a blend of excitement and fear. One of the women in the group asked me, "What are you worried about as you go through this process?" I barely had to think, "What if the book is not a good book?" I had put my heart and soul into that project. I was excited about the completion of the book. But what if no one else liked it? What if women would be forced to share a kind—but not truthful—nod that they enjoyed the book and found it helpful?

I know I'm not alone. Many women don't even start working toward their biggest dream for fear that they could never do it—and if they tried it would not be any good. How many times have you allowed fear of failure to hold you back? Any time we're growing and stretching ourselves out of our comfort zone, we are bound to feel fear and uncertainty.

**Many women don't even start working toward their biggest dream for fear that they could never do it—and if they tried it would not be any good.**

We have two choices where fear is concerned: 1) we can choose to not do anything because of our fear, or 2) we can do it afraid.

Which will you choose?

5. **Be kind to yourself in the process.**

One of the women who joined the Women Who Spark Tribe on Facebook came for encouragement. She said, "I'm tired of quitting things before I even get started."

Getting started and keeping going is a challenge most of us have experienced.

I've shared some things about Ellen's journey across the bridge. She's made amazing progress. But that doesn't mean it's been easy. She reached out to me a couple of weeks ago feeling overwhelmed by the number of things coming at her every day. Part of her overwhelm was created because, at the same time she's dealing with everyday life, she is on the bridge moving toward her new land. She was feeling guilty by the need to set some of her goals on the back burner.

We have to be careful when emotions suddenly hit us in the middle of working toward a better future, because our belief in ourselves can go spiraling downhill fast. Voices in our heads start to say: "I can't do it." "It's too much." "See, I was right. There is too much going on in my life to think about what I want."

I told Ellen, "Give yourself permission to pause for a time. Focus on the things that life is presenting to you. When things calm down, and when you're ready, you can start to make forward progress again." She needed that permission. And you know what, I'm proud of Ellen for getting on her bridge, even if she needs to take a short pit stop.

Some women will stop short of even getting on the bridge. They think, "It will take so long to do what I want to do." Consider this: whether you are on the bridge making slow, steady progress toward your dreams or not on the bridge at all, the same amount of time is going to pass. A decade from now, do you want to be on the bridge to the new land—or perhaps already in the new land? Or do you want to deal with the regret of never starting?

You can do anything you set your mind to. But, remember to be kind to yourself in the process. If you're on track, great. If you're off track, still great. Experiencing a win today? Fantastic. Experienced a setback? That's okay, too. This is all part of the journey.

If you're realistic about your progress, it will be easier to be kind to yourself.

## Let's Get Real About the Tough Stuff

It's hard to believe in yourself when you spend most of your time each day in a negative environment. Joan L.

Turley knows exactly how that feels, "I was 40 years old and working in an academic setting. I felt so insignificant. They had no problem letting me know to keep my mouth shut."

That was 23 years ago.

Today Joan, the author of *Sacred Work in Secular Places: Finding Joy In The Workplace,*[6] is 63 years old and one of the most positive, kind, and loving women I know. She is launching a new business—one that leverages an extreme talent discovered along her unexpected journey.

Joan told me, "At one point in my life I was confident. Then, in 1988, when I was 31 years old—following 12 years in a soul-crushing ministry—I had a nervous breakdown." She continued, "I had a complete loss of belief. I didn't know who I was. I longed to make a difference in the world even though I no longer felt I had anything to contribute."

Joan then stepped into her first secular job ever, working for a school district. She told me, "I was the copy girl. I had no formal education. I believed my life would never be more than making copies in a school room."

Thankfully, belief started to grow in Joan's heart again. It was sparked by what Joan calls "an Ebenezer moment." "God spoke to me and told me to start meeting with him in the mornings. I did." Joan said. "As I met with God, I started to write in my journal. One of my entries was, *'I want to write and speak.'*"

Within six months, Joan's life started to change. "I was 43 years old. I went to work for the president of a communications firm as her executive assistant. As I started writing some things for her, she declared one day, 'I thought I hired an executive assistant, but I've hired a copywriter!'"

Things began to look up for Joan.

From there, she went on to work for the president of a non-profit as her executive assistant and ended up becoming the director of community relations.

Joan says those were the two hardest jobs of her life, and they got her ready for what was coming next.

> At age 48, I walked into a salon and day spa in Houston, TX. My former boss told them, 'You need Joan.' I came in as a support person, and six months later, when the director of operations quit, Francie, the owner, told me, "You're it." I told her, No, no, no. You don't understand, I've never been a first. I've always been a second. Francie told Joan, "No, you're it."

That moment would test Joan's belief in herself. It also pushed her to discover new capabilities

Joan had never read a balance sheet, led a team, hired anyone, or fired a soul. And, she was the new Director of Operations. Joan told me this is proof that God never wastes our waiting, sorrows, or sufferings.

Joan held that job for ten years, and today she is starting a consulting business to teach salon owners how to maximize their business and their profits. Joan's message to salon owners?

> *Hey there, weary and worn salon owner, I'm looking for you. I know it's been hard, but don't give up brave soul. Help is on the way.*

Joan is on fire. She is 63 years old and starting this brand-new journey, leveraging skills she never planned to have. She told me, "If Colonel Sanders could start KFC at age 60, I can start this business at age 63."

## Joan's advice to you:

Your life may not look like what you imagined in your 20s and 30s. I am proof that one thing can lead to another. God is in the business of moving through people regardless of their level of education. He is in the business of partnership with us wherever we are. He is never limited by the *not enoughs* in our lives. All that is required is a heart to serve. My prayer has long been, *"Lord, will you put people in my life who are further along in their journey than I am?"*

**Chapter Highlights**

**Chapter 1: Is There More to Life Than This?**

- Get clear about what is nagging at you, feels unresolved, and needs your attention.

**Chapter 2: Let's Get a Few Things Straight**

- You have a runway ahead of you for the second half of your life and can change your beliefs about what lies ahead.

**Chapter 3: The Sparks Have Dimmed**

- Many mid-life women experience apathy. You can treasure the memories in your positive bucket and do the work to leave the negative bucket of memories behind.

**Chapter 4: Clean Up the Things That Matter to You**

- When you look around, what do you notice? As you assess ten areas of your life, what areas need to be cleaned up? Which need to be reignited and reinvented?

**Chapter 5: Women Who Took Action to Clean Up the Mess**

- A bridge connects the old land to the new land. You don't have to have a clear picture of your new land to step onto the bridge.

**Chapter 6: It's Time to Reignite and Reinvent**

- You may very well have three, four or five decades left, and you have a choice to settle for where you're at, reignite or reinvent.

**Chapter 7: Design Your 80-Year Old Self**

- Envision a lovely woman you know who is in her 80s and think about your own 80-year-old self.

**Chapter 8: Inspiration From Women in Their 70s, 80s, and 90s**

- You can be fully alive in the later years of your life.

**Chapter 9: Believe in Yourself**

- Belief precedes action.
- Your belief in yourself is determined by you.
- Five ways to start believing in yourself include:
    1. Believe it's possible.
    2. Create a vision of what it looks like.
    3. Think more about your past successes than your past failures.
    4. Accept fear as a predictable part of your journey.
    5. Be kind to yourself in the process.

# CHAPTER 10

## Transform Yourself for Action

*Trying to do it all and expecting it all can be done exactly right is a recipe for disappointment. Perfection is the enemy.*

~ Cheryl Sandberg, COO, Facebook

If you've traveled by plane, you've heard the pilots speak through the intercom and say, "Flight attendants, prepare for takeoff."

Have you ever thought about what that involves?

There is an entire checklist of things the flight attendants need to do to prepare the passengers and the cabin to safely jet off 30,000 feet into the sky: ensure the luggage is properly stowed, check that everyone is wearing their seatbelt, instruct passengers to put phones in airplane mode, chat with the passengers in the exit rows to ensure they can throw an emergency door "out the window" if needed, make sure everyone knows how to operate their oxygen mask, and inform us that we can float on our seat cushions if we crash into the sea.

Even before this, the pilots have worked through their preparation checklists.

What about you? As you prepare to jet off into your amazing future you need a checklist, too. If you don't have your checklist already, let's get to work!

As you read through the rest of this chapter, you'll work through a checklist to prepare yourself for action. The key here is preparation. The actual framework for *action taking* will start in Chapter 11.

This checklist is designed to position you to experience greater confidence, happiness, and a clear purpose in your coming decades.

You'll notice lots of checkboxes along the way. I've also compiled everything into one neat list at the end of this chapter so you can see a condensed version of what this chapter contains at-a-glance.

Let's get started! Buckle your seatbelt, because you have work to do.

## Preliminary Steps to Prepare for Action

1. **Acknowledge that you have time.**

I've talked about this at length. A core concept that I have woven into Women Who Spark After 50 is that we should be leaning into our 80-year old selves. And beyond. Even if you are in your 50s, 60s, or 70s, you have a lot of life to live.

Do not let your past define you. Even if your past feels like one disappointment after another, your past is behind you, and you have these decades of life in front of you.

Think about these examples of people living their lives fully in their last decades:

- Queen Elizabeth is 94 years old and still actively serving as Queen after 65 years on the throne.
- Mother Teresa served the sick and poor until she died at age 87.
- Ruth Bader Ginsberg became a Supreme Court Justice when she was 60 years old and served until her death at age 87.
- Betty White is 97 years old and has been acting for 80 years.
- Mary Kay Ash started Mary Kay Cosmetics when she was 45 years old and was involved with her company until her death at age 82.
- Colonel Sanders was 65 years old when he started Kentucky Fried Chicken. (I know he's a guy, but I LOVE that he was 65.)
- Are you in?

☐ Yes! I acknowledge that I have a lot of years ahead of me.

2. **Create a vision for your future.**

Reinvention later in life can be scary. Especially if you've walked a fairly traditional path by working for someone else or taking time off to raise kids. Many women, however, still want to make a bigger impact. They want to change people's lives. The challenge can be in not knowing how. A common refrain I hear is, "I don't want to keep doing what I'm doing, but I have no idea what I'll do next."

You created a vision board earlier in the book for your 80-year old self. Grab that. (Or get busy and do it now if you skipped it earlier.)

You already know what your 80-year old self looks like and is doing. Now let's move closer to the present time. Think about one, five, or ten years from now. Can you connect with a passion? Do you have something that has been percolating within you?

What ideas are you thinking about?

Sometimes the best way to create a concept for your future is to page through magazines to see what grabs your attention. Starting with a blank slate, along with nothing more than your own thoughts, may not work.

As you leaf through magazines, note what looks appealing to you:

- Starting a non-profit.
- Volunteering at a hospital.
- Working with small children.
- Rock climbing.
- Becoming a tour guide on the bourbon trail.
- Opening a small retail shop.
- Getting into better shape.
- Traveling the world.
- Becoming a tour guide.

- Visiting all of the national parks.
- Joining the Peace Corps.
- Writing a book.
- Going back to school for an entirely new career.
- Getting a certificate or a technical degree.

☐ Yes, I'm doing the work. I'll create a vision board for what my future is going to look like.

3. **Start a SPARK Box.**

In 2006, I knew I wanted to write a book and support women on the journey to experience greater happiness. However, I didn't have much more to work with than that concept.

I stood solidly on the old land, with one foot on the bridge. I knew I would one day cross that bridge to a new land where I would do this work. My desire to discover what the new land held for me led me to discover the concept of a "Spark Box." I found a sturdy white box at the store with a lift-off lid and, because I was writing a book, labeled it "Book Box."

With no timeline in mind, I started throwing things in the box. If I read an article that resonated with me, I ripped it out and threw it in my book box. If I had an idea while I was out and about, I wrote it on a napkin or sticky note and threw it in the book box. I also started filling up journals. These were, however, chronicling the tough stuff—the fears, insecurities, regrets, and shame. Each time I filled up a journal—you guessed it—I threw it into the book box.

My friend Ellen, who is returning to her passion for make-up, is starting a business to help women over

50 learn how to apply make-up. She has some pretty cool and exciting ideas. She liked my book box idea, so she went out and found a pretty flip-top box and labeled it her "Passion Box." She called it that because her makeup business is her new passion.

If there's something you know you want to go after, start a Spark Box to throw things in the box that support your idea.

Not sure exactly what you want to work toward? That's okay, too. Your Spark Box will have a broader purpose. I suggest you throw anything at all in your Spark Box that lights a spark within you. Bring a collision of ideas into one box. As you one day dump them out to sort through them, you may find a theme that sparks an idea for your future passion project or purpose.

What do you think? Can you envision how a Spark Box will help you?

- ☐ A Spark Box? Absolutely! I'm on it. I'll start shopping right now.

4. **Find a mentor who is 10, 20 or 30 years older than you.**

Look around.

Do you see women—10, 20, or 30 years older than you—inspiring you?

I have a neighbor across the street. She is in her 70s and a widow. She and her husband started a business a number of years ago, and she now runs the company along with her son. I have another neighbor who is running her non-profit organization, and she is well into her 80s. I admire these women who wake up every day, get dressed, put on their make-up, and back out of their garages at 7:30 am to head into the world to make a difference.

I'm inspired by both of these women because I envision continuing to have an impact professionally in my 70s and 80s.

As I write this, I have not honed in on who my mentor will be for my 80-year-old self. I'm on the lookout for her.

Like me, are you interested in finding someone to emulate? If you are, who are you looking for? I encourage you to find someone who is doing something that resonates with your vision of your 80-year old self.

- If you want to be the most amazing grandma—and matriarch to your family—find a woman who is already doing that.
- If you want to start a new business in your 50s, 60s, or 70s, can you find a woman who did that?
- Do you aspire to have an active lifestyle with a focus on volunteerism? Okay, you know the mentor you want to find.

A mentor is someone you can talk to every couple of months to gather inspiration from her journey, specifically through her storytelling.

If you decide you'd like to ask someone to be your mentor, it may be helpful to describe what you envision. You might say something like this:

> I admire you as I've gotten to know you. As I look ahead to my future, I could see myself doing some of the same things you're doing and enjoying life in the ways I see you enjoying life. I'm interested in having a mentor, someone who can help me navigate through these next couple of decades

of my journey. Would you be willing to be that person? Perhaps join me for a cup of coffee and a chat every couple of months?

When you meet with your mentor, be sure to have a few questions in mind. Your question may relate to an area where you feel stuck. For example, "I'd love to take a couple of classes at the technical college, but I am afraid I'll feel out of place given my age. Have you had experiences where you've been the oldest person in the room?" Or you can ask a more open-ended question like, "Tell me about a difficult season you've navigated through in your life."

- ☐ Yes, I love it! I'm going to start looking for a mentor.

5. **Begin to have conversations with other women you meet on your journey.**

You may love the idea of having a mentor.

If you have one, that's fantastic.

In addition to your mentor, you will be surrounded by, and cross paths with, many amazing, lovely, sparkly women

As you consider your future life, you may not yet have clarity about what you want to do with these coming decades. And even if you do have clarity, there is so much we can learn from other women. I encourage you to talk with women you already know, as well as women you sit next to at luncheons and wedding receptions.

Ask them what they're doing today, as well as what they've done throughout their lives. Your curiosity will convince them to open the floodgates for more information about their sparkly life journeys. You're bound to find inspiration in the nooks and crannies of their stories.

My cousin, Mandy, recently decided to conduct a series of interviews with her 96-year-old mother to learn more about her life. She is having so much fun and learning things she never knew. Her mom is also loving the process. After the first interview, her mom sat down to create an outline for their future interviews so she wouldn't leave anything out.

This is working two ways: Mandy is learning things about her mom that are inspiring her own journey, and this process is bringing her mom a lot of joy.

I recall that in my childhood, my grandpa had such an interest in telling his life stories. I am so sorry to say I didn't pay attention at the time. I'd give anything to go back in time and journal the things he told me.

- ☐ Yes, I'm ready to listen! The women around me, even strangers, have potential to inspire me. I'll be more proactive in my conversations.

6. **Enhance the Brand of YOU.**

Buckle up for this section. You have work to do.

Personal brand was not a thing when I started my adult life. We went about our lives, but we didn't pause to think about "What brand do I want to convey?" And, in fact, many of us likely did some harm to our brand because we weren't thinking about it.

So, what is a personal brand?

No different from a company brand, really. It is the perception or impression others have of you, based upon your experiences, competencies, achievements and perhaps, most important of all, your actions.

Your brand is the accumulation of all of the things you say and do. (Not to mention all the things you've already said and done in the past.) Your reputation is an element of your brand.

In this section, I'd like to pose nine areas for you to consider as comprising the "Brand of You." As you look at each area, consider where you are now, how you've shown up in this area over the years, and what you'd like to do differently in the future.

I've seen women stand taller by simply getting intentional about these things—and fixing areas that need fixing. Or, at least, improving or reframing how they show up in life.

**a) Your overall view on life**

I'm so grateful for my grandma who consistently framed my thinking in life when I was young with "Everything will be okay," and "They're doing the best they can." These two mantras covered both situations and people. My grandma was gracious, hard-working, non-judgmental, and patient.

She instilled within me:

- The situation will be okay.
- The people mean well.

My dad overlayed that with, "You can do whatever you want in life."

These three things work together to create a positive overall view of life.

What does your view look like?

Situations:

- ☐ I tend to be optimistic.
- ☐ I tend to be pessimistic.

Other people:

- ☐ I'm gracious and know people mean well.
- ☐ I'm more critical and don't always trust positive intentions.

Your own life:

- ☐ I have faith that I can do whatever I want.
- ☐ I don't have faith in myself.

As people think about your presence, would they say you light up a room when you enter, or do you bring some gray clouds with you?

**b) The role learning plays in your life.**

Mandy, who has been interviewing her 96-year old mom to make sure she captures the details of her life, told me, "While my mom regrets not getting a formal college education, she is one of the smartest people I know. She reads incessantly."

The truth is, you don't need to be enrolled in a school to learn every day. Information surrounds us. What are you listening to and reading?

Whether you prefer to read or watch TV, you can learn from others through biographies and documentaries.

Are you prepared to have stimulating, intellectual conversations as you move through your later years?

You also have plenty of opportunities to take classes, both online and at your local community college. What do you want to learn? The options are endless: learn a second language, dust off your piano playing skills, develop a new talent in the kitchen, take up knitting, become a professional proofreader, finish a college degree you started years ago, learn the game of baseball, or study wines.

You get to choose and there is no wrong answer.

How do you want to engage with your adult children and grandchildren? How do you want to participate in conversations when you attend events? How interesting and informed do you want to be?

- ☐ I'm in! I'll keep learning as I continue my life journey.

**c) Your confidence and sense of self-worth.**

We've talked about this already at length. Life has a way of chipping away at confidence and self-worth. As you look ahead, the loss of these attributes does not have to remain a part of your brand.

As I was interviewing women for this book, one story grabbed my attention. Cyndy Keller, at age 69, accepted an invitation to lead a networking group in a new community she had moved to a year earlier. She told me, "The process of putting this together has boosted my confidence and increased my feelings of self-worth."

Confidence is a skill anyone can develop at any age.

That is because self-worth is a subjective value of our worth. Ultimately, we decide how we see ourselves. Most often our perspective is influenced by things people have said to us and experiences we've had in life that didn't go the way we wanted. However, it is possible to shift your thinking from "I am not enough" to "I am enough."

**It is possible to shift your thinking from "I am not enough" to "I am enough."**

The first step is deciding what you want. You can declare it here.

- ☐ "I want to be confident."
- ☐ "I want to feel a sense of self-worth."
- ☐ "I'm willing to do the work."

**d) Your connection to fear and perfectionism.**

Similar to the ones above—confidence and self-worth—fear and perfectionism are choices.

I'm not suggesting it's easy to overcome being afraid or that it's easy to set your perfectionism aside. But I am suggesting you don't have to drag them along through your life like balls and chains attached to your ankles.

Fear holds women back. Plain and simple.

What will people think?

What if I fail?

And perfectionism? It fuels fear. If we have a belief that things have to be perfect in order to take a step or move in the direction of a dream, fear will jump in and tell us that we'd better wait until we're sure.

Certainty is fleeting. The possibility of feeling certainty in most areas of our lives is rarely 100%. This is where risk taking comes into play, combined with a mindset of "good enough" and conviction that, "It doesn't matter what other people think."

I remember my agony over what to do when I was embroiled in a complete mess of a second marriage. I thought, *If I end a marriage again, what will people think?* I was paralyzed by the fear of people judging me negatively. When I finally took the risk, I didn't feel a moment of judgment from anyone. Support and encouragement came from all around me.

Similarly, I know women who won't take a chance on their dreams because of a blend of fear and perfectionism. They tell themselves, "I'll stick with what's safe and with what I know."

Let me give you a friendly warning: This may end up being one of your biggest regrets.

I read something that fascinated me several years ago. In the short term, women regret what they've done, as well as certain choices they made. In the long term, women regret what they didn't do with their lives. How do you want your future 80-year-old self to look back on what you're doing today?

**In the long term, women regret what they didn't do with their lives.**

- ☐ Okay. Another thing for me to take a look at. I'll explore moving away from fear and perfectionism. (Spoiler alert: you don't have to know how you're going to do it, only that you want to do it.)

e) **Your wardrobe, hair and makeup.**

Whew! Let's move on to something a bit lighter, away from our headspace.

The messy middle of life may afford us just enough time to get dressed, blow dry our hair, and throw on some makeup. And many women pull this together nicely. Others never quite get to it given all of the demands of the whirlwind of life: kids, job, household, bills, volunteering, planning, shopping, and cooking.

Years ago, I knew one of the moms in my kids' school on a waving basis. What I recall is that she almost always wore mom jeans (no judgment here!), dark baggy t-shirts, and clogs. She whipped her hair up in a ponytail and didn't bother with make-up. She often looked sad, and she rarely spoke. I think it would be fair to say most women didn't really notice when she walked into a room.

Somewhere along the way, she experienced an unwanted divorce. Some time went by, and I didn't see her. I don't think I realized I wasn't seeing her until one day she walked into a meeting at school. And, wow! She had dropped 20 pounds, she had a stylish haircut, her make-up was beautiful, and she was wearing a fitted, colorful outfit. The most important part of all of this was her smile and her posture. She held her head high. You could see the confidence in her. From this point forward, each time I saw her, she was engaging in conversations, sparkling and showing up differently.

Whatever your journey has been in this regard, you have time to explore and define your style. Fashion is what gets presented to us in the external world, relative to available clothing and accessories. Style is how you define yourself—it's how you pull it all together.

What do you want to do with your hair? Look at photos of women who may be your age or older. What have they done with their hair that is catching your attention? Are they shifting to short? Are they drawing out a beautiful tone of gray?

What about your fashion choices? Is it time to step aside from your steady menu of jeans and t-shirts? Do you need to introduce color into your wardrobe? Do you love scarves but feel unsure how to accessorize with them? Do you even know what looks good on you?

Now, on to makeup. I'm intrigued by what my friend Ellen told me about make-up considerations while we were on a walk recently. She specializes in helping women over 50 learn how to apply make-up. We can learn to avoid the make-up faux pas that actually make us look older and even do some magic around our eyes to offset sleepy eyelids. We get to choose whether we will continue into our older years splashing on some foundation, topped off with a swoosh of blush, or if we'll learn some new techniques that will make us stand out as *women who spark*.

☐ Hmmm, I'm intrigued. I'll add hair, makeup, and wardrobe to my list.

**f) Your teeth.**

Yes, this deserves its own attention. Women who have stained or crooked teeth may experience lower confidence in social settings. Why? They are less likely to smile, and the very act of trying to hide their teeth will inhibit their confidence in entering into the conversation. This, in turn, may impact their self-esteem.

Once we reach mid-life, it may be the perfect time to think about replacing a mouth full of silver fillings with porcelain-colored fillings, invest in teeth straightening, and commit to a teeth-whitening regime.

While most women will not think twice about remodeling a kitchen or repainting the whole house, they forget some of the attention they personally need.

- ☐ As a matter of fact, my teeth do need some attention.

**g) Your weight.**

Just as teeth deserve special consideration, weight does, too. I could have talked about this issue in our next section of health and fitness, but women's obsession and dissatisfaction with weight is often all-consuming.

You may recall the serious conversation my sister's doctor had with her. Sherri had given weight-loss attention her entire adult life, but this is the first time she buckled down, took it on as a change-in-lifestyle initiative, and took care of it. She dropped 30 lbs. in three months (through a healthy approach), feels more energetic, and no longer experiences chronic pain. She has an exhilarating sense of freedom every day.

The biggest thing Sherri realized was that she couldn't keep doing what she'd always done and expect to lose weight. Her transformation required major lifestyle changes and a huge amount of commitment. Today she'll tell you it was absolutely worth giving up all sugar and walking six miles a day.

It's certainly not easy, but that's why weight loss is a $70+ billion-dollar-per-year industry. You have many options to explore and consider. The question for you will boil down to, "Am I ready to do the hard work, make the sacrifices, and say 'no' to the things I want?" How important is it for you to, once and for all, feel good about your weight?

It's on the list, because it's part of your brand. What do you envision in terms of your size as you move into your future decades? Do you need to shed some pounds?

☐ Yessssss. I need it on my list.

**h) Your health and fitness.**

What kind of lifestyle will you commit to?

Thinking about what you put in your cart at the grocery store is a great place to start. The food you choose to eat, the amount of food you consume, and your consumption of water versus soda and sugary drinks all play a key role in the type of lifestyle you will lead.

Some other critical factors include the amount of sleep you get at night and the number of minutes you spend moving and exercising each day. (Also, consider the lifestyle choices that will affect the preceding list, such as how many hours you spend binge-watching TV each week.)

The most important thing to keep in mind is that your overall health—across the decades—will be a result of the micro-habits you commit to every day.

Remember Janet Black? You read about her in Chapter 6. She came off all of her meds in her 50s. Every one of them. Inspired by the book, *Miracle Morning*,[7] she got serious about adopting habits that changed the trajectory of her health for the rest of her life.

In the fall, I met a lovely woman named Amy. She shared her dismay about gaining 30 pounds during menopause. She said, "I'm just so discouraged. I've never had this difficulty with my weight, and I feel terrible." In January, she and her husband committed to Whole30 for three rounds over 90 days. She lost the 30 pounds.

When Sherri gave up sugar, she got way more than she could have imagined. Recently she told me, "I just realized something. I've gotten my athletic self back again." When Sherri was a kid, she was a competitive swimmer and basketball player. She qualified for the Junior Olympics. Her stroke was butterfly—and she was a powerhouse.

Now, 35 years later, she is rediscovering that part of her identity. Her muscle tone is back, and she said, "I can't believe how small my legs have gotten." Sure enough, a recent photo showed her wearing a pair of cute little shorts unlike anything I've seen her in for over 20 years!

You, too, have choices. You can regain a state of health and fitness that has slipped away.

You don't have to simply accept an identity created by life circumstances such as, "I'm an overweight woman." Or, "I'm a woman who has to be on these meds." Or, "I'm a woman who needs to live with chronic pain."

Begin by deciding who you want to be. Envision it.

If you can dream it, you can achieve it. It may not be easy, but anything is possible.

Envision *what* you want.

☐ I'll do what it takes!

**i) Your interpersonal communication style**

I like this one.

While interpersonal communication is a big topic, I'm going to talk about only two things in this section: 1) what you talk about and 2) the conviction of your opinions.

I'll explain.

Do you talk about ideas or other people? When you talk about other people, do you focus on the good or gossip about the things you don't like? As part of your brand, are you known as a positive gracious person or a gossip?

Which do you prefer?

When you share your opinions, do you share to persuade or do you share to add? Sharing to persuade suggests others should see things the same way you do. It suggests right and wrong.

Or do you add your opinions to the conversation and accept that others are as welcome to their opinions as you are to yours? While there are times when we need to stand up for something we know is right, most of the time we gain more by taking time to understand others and gaining perspective that will help improve our relationships.

The strength of your opinions will influence how you interact with your family and friends. It is something I'll share a bit more about in our next "Brand of You" section: "Define Your Role as Mom and Grandma."

- ☐ Ah jeez, I could lighten up about my opinions.

The "Brand of You" is a big category. If you're feeling overwhelmed at the moment, it's okay to pause.

One of the things you hear me say over and over again is to not do everything at once.

### j) Define your role as a mom and grandma

If you are a mom, it's likely your years of intense parenting are coming to an end. Your children may be out in the adult world as you're reading this—or close to launching.

Now is the time to think about your future role. What kind of mom do you want to be for your adult children? Considering all of the tense relationships that exist, it is worth your while to give this topic serious consideration.

I see women who are too involved in the lives of their adult children. I know many of our happiest times are when we're with our children. Or maybe we should say when they are with us. But let's get clear about something: They are not responsible for our happiness. They should not have to shoulder the burden of keeping us entertained or of even being a priority to them. Adult children have their lives to live. They have their own children—or may eventually have their own.

I will speak for a moment on behalf of my blended family of five adult children. Along with their significant others, this is a group of 10 adults, many of them with multiple sets of parents. My son, Ben, and his wife, Kelsey, have four sets of parents (and eventually grandparents) to visit on holidays, among other things. The last thing I will do to them is put pressure on them to fit me in at a time that is convenient for me.

That doesn't mean I don't want them in every one of my holiday celebrations, because I'd lock up all of these kids in our home for every single holiday if I could have my way. But this isn't about me. The message my husband and I have decided to send to all of our children is this, "We love you all, and our home is always open to you. We are happy when you're here. But there is no pressure. As you fit together your schedules, we'll share timeframes with you, and if they work, fantastic. If they don't work, we have 355 days a year that are non-competing days."

In contrast, I've seen women pout, lay on the guilt, and play the "If you really loved me" card. No. This is not the best brand for you.

What about your role as a grandma?

I hadn't thought about a specific scenario until a few years ago. Some friends of ours told their married children, "Just so we're all on the same page about this, we will help you with your kids occasionally—for date nights and get-away weekends—but we will not be your kids' babysitters. So, don't even ask."

Wow.

It's good to know what you are planning. It's also good to know what your kids want.

What kind of mom and grandma do you want to be?

- ☐ A needy mom whose happiness is tied to time with my adult children.
- ☐ A mom who finds happiness in my own life and whose time with adult children is a bonus.
- ☐ A mom who places guilt on my adult children when they don't spend enough time with me.
- ☐ A mom who understands my adult children have several priorities in life to juggle.
- ☐ A kind, gracious grandma who will be available in the way my kids would like me to be.
- ☐ A needy grandma who will pout if my kids and grandkids don't make me enough of a priority.
- ☐ A grandma who will sneak my grandchildren sugar against their parents' wishes.
- ☐ A grandma who will honor the wishes of my children in their roles as parents.

- ☐ A busy grandma who will do the best I can to be available for my grandchildren.
- ☐ A babysitting grandma who wants to be the childcare solution for my grandchildren.
- ☐ An opinionated grandma who will coach the parents on how to raise their children.
- ☐ What else is on your mind about the kind of grandma you're going to be?
- ☐ Write it down here:________________
  __________________________________

This is too important a season to leave it to chance.

- ☐ Yes. I'll give thought in advance to how I'll be showing up as a mom and grandma.

**k) Make some advance decisions about technology.**

For years, I've felt sad that my dad and stepmom never stepped up to figure out technology.

Today they have 16 grandchildren and nine great grandchildren, and they are not in regular contact with any of them. Some contact, yes. Regular contact, no.

My parents can't text or email. They never learned how. As a result, the only way they can communicate with their grandchildren and great grandchildren is by a telephone call, a card or letter in the mail, or an in-person visit.

You can imagine how much they've missed out on seeing and experiencing over the years.

They started waving the white flag of confusion years ago. Can you relate?

Make no mistake. Technology will pass us by unless we make keeping up a priority.

I encourage you to decide in advance that connectivity to your family and to the world is important enough that you will make the effort to stay current.

- ☐ Yes! I'm on it. Technology will not leave me behind.

What else do you need to do to set yourself up for action?

- ☐ Yes, I know I need to get after this one: ___ ______________________________

Whew! THAT was a lot.

Seriously.

Don't fret if you feel overwhelmed. In this chapter, you're simply creating a roadmap so you know the direction you need to go to create the future you want. The rest of the book will help you get started on that journey.

In this chapter, instead of a tough stuff story, we're ending with a checklist so you can think about the tough stuff *you* need to sort through. You probably answered the questions along the way, but here it is in one neat, tidy place so you can really think through what you need to focus on.

If you'd like, you can also download this checklist at www.womenwhosparkbooks.com.

I know this is hard, but you owe it to yourself to do the work.

**Summary Checklist for Chapter 10: Transform Yourself for Action**

This checklist is a summary of all of the things you've considered throughout Chapter 10. Here it is in one tidy place.

**Preliminary steps for action:**

- ☐ Yes! I acknowledge that I have a lot of years ahead of me.
- ☐ Yes, I'm doing the work. I'll create a vision board for what my future is going to look like.
- ☐ A Spark Box? Absolutely! I'm on it. I'll start shopping right now.
- ☐ Yes, I love it! I'm going to start looking for a mentor.
- ☐ Yes, I'm ready to listen! The women around me, even strangers, have potential to inspire me. I'll be more proactive in my conversations.
- ☐ I'm ready to work on the Brand of Me.

**My overall view of life:**

Situations:

- ☐ I tend to be optimistic.
- ☐ I tend to be pessimistic.

Other people:

- ☐ I'm gracious and know people mean well.
- ☐ I'm more critical and don't always trust that people have positive intentions.

My own life:

- ☐ I have faith that I can do whatever I want.
- ☐ I don't have faith in myself.

**The role learning plays in my life:**

- ☐ I'm in. I'll keep learning as I continue my life journey.

**My confidence and sense of self-worth:**

- ☐ "I want to be confident."
- ☐ "I want to feel a sense of self-worth."
- ☐ "I'm willing to do the work."

**My connection to fear and perfectionism:**

- ☐ Okay. This is another thing for me to take a look at. I'll explore moving away from fear and perfectionism. (Spoiler alert: you don't have to know how you're going to do it, only that you want to do it.)

**My wardrobe, hair and make-up:**

- ☐ Hmmm, I'm intrigued. I'll add hair, make-up and wardrobe to my list.

**My teeth:**

- ☐ As a matter of fact, my teeth do need some attention.

**My weight:**

- ☐ Yessssss. I need it on my list.

**My health and fitness:**

- ☐ I'm in! I need to step up and do the work to regain my health and fitness.

**My interpersonal communication style:**

- ☐ Ah jeez, I could lighten up about my opinions.

**My role as a mom and grandma:**

What kind of mom and grandma do I want to be?

- ☐ A needy mom whose happiness is tied to time with my adult children.
- ☐ A mom who finds happiness in her own life and whose time with adult children is a bonus.
- ☐ A mom who places guilt on my adult children when they don't spend enough time with me.
- ☐ A mom who understands my adult children have several priorities in life to juggle.
- ☐ A kind, gracious grandma who will be available in the way my kids would like me to be.
- ☐ A needy grandma who will pout if my kids and grandkids don't make me enough of a priority.
- ☐ A supportive grandma who will follow the wishes of the parents.

- ☐ A grandma who will sneak my grandchildren sugar against the request of their parents.
- ☐ A grandma who will honor the wishes of my children in their role as parents.
- ☐ A busy grandma who will do the best I can to be available for my grandchildren.
- ☐ A babysitting grandma who wants to be the childcare solution for my grandchildren.
- ☐ An opinionated grandma who will coach the parents on how to raise their children.
- ☐ What else is on your mind about the kind of grandma you're going to be?
- ☐ Write it down here:______________________

This is too important a season to leave it to chance.

- ☐ Yes. I'll give thought in advance to how I'll be showing up as a mom and grandma.

**Make some advance decisions about technology:**

- ☐ Yes! I'm on it. Technology will not leave me behind.

**What else?**

- ☐ What else do you need to do to set yourself up for action?

## Chapter Highlights

**Chapter 1: Is There More to Life Than This?**

- Get clear about what is nagging at you, feels unresolved, and needs your attention.

**Chapter 2: Let's get a few things straight**

- You have a runway ahead of you for the second half of your life and can change your beliefs about what lies ahead.

**Chapter 3: The Sparks Have Dimmed**

- Many mid-life women experience apathy. You can treasure the memories in your positive bucket and do the work to leave the negative bucket of memories behind.

**Chapter 4: Clean Up The Things That Matter To You**

- When you look around, what do you notice? As you assess ten areas of your life, what areas need to be cleaned up? Which need to be reignited and reinvented?

**Chapter 5: Women Who Took Action To Clean Up The Mess**

- A bridge connects the old land to the new land. You don't have to have a clear picture of your new land to step onto the bridge.

**Chapter 6: It's Time to Reignite and Reinvent**

- You may very well have three, four or five decades left, and you have a choice to settle for where you're at, reignite or reinvent.

**Chapter 7: Design Your 80-Year Old Self**

- Envision a lovely woman you know who is in her 80s, and think about your own 80-year-old self.

**Chapter 8: Inspiration From Women in Their 70s, 80s, and 90s**

- You can be fully alive in the later years of your life.

**Chapter 9: Believe in Yourself**

- Belief precedes action, Your belief in yourself is determined by you.

**Chapter 10: Transform Yourself for Action**

Steps to Prepare for Action:

- Acknowledge that you have time.
- Create a vision for your future.
- Start a SPARK Box.
- Find a mentor who is 10 – 30 years older than you.
- Begin to have conversations with other women you meet on your journey.
- Enhance the brand of you.

# CHAPTER 11

## Get Started. Where Are YOU Going?

*You don't have to be great to start, but you have to start to be great.*

~ Zig Ziglar

Are you ready to get started? What does that look like? After all the work you've done up to this point in the book, are you wondering if it's even possible?

Let me tell you a story about what getting started can look like—and how major life challenges can serve as inspiration.

My dear friend Nancy and I have been business partners of our leadership development company—Living As A Leader—for 25 years. Nancy is a consummate professional and an amazing human being in more ways than I can count. She is talented in her field of work, makes a significant impact in every client organization she supports, and is a great curriculum designer for our company. She is friendly, interested, and articulate.

We've been through a lot of ups and downs together, and we've been there for one another. We've seen each other's kids grow up, she supported me through two divorces, and I supported her through one. We've had good years and bad years in business. We've had great friend moments and some knockdown, drag out fights as business partners.

While Nancy is an amazing woman in about one gazillion ways, it is the role she serves as the single mom of Amanda and Lyndsay that is most remarkable. Lyndsay, age 27, is taking the world by storm. She moved to New York a year ago to pursue her professional career in choreography and dance. Amanda is Nancy's special needs daughter. God hand-picked Nancy to be her mom. This is recognized by every person who knows Nancy and Amanda. Amanda is a sweet, lovely 21-year-old girl who has autism. If we could put a period at the end of that sentence and be done, the story would be less remarkable than what it is.

It doesn't end there. Amanda is complex, and the full spectrum of her challenges remains undiagnosed. As a young adult, she is non-verbal and unable to take care of her own basic needs. Nancy dresses her, showers her, and spoon-feeds her meals. Because of Amanda's inability to chew her food and difficulty swallowing her food—as well as her body's response to food, in general—Amanda eats a carefully selected menu of only pureed foods. Her diet primarily consists of yogurt, pudding, SpaghettiOs, and pureed peanut butter and jelly sandwiches, blended with cranberry juice. Oh, and she loves ice cream.

Nancy's care team is comprised of women (from college age to middle age) who are specially trained to take care of Amanda. Nancy, at age 60, is unable to move freely about her life like most of us, because arranging care for Amanda is a constant companion in Nancy's day. This co-exists with need-to-be-home curfews on any given day.

When it comes to the messy middles of life, Nancy has navigated through more than most women. Yet, she is gracious, feels blessed to be Amanda's and Lyndsay's mom, and adores both of her daughters infinitely.

Nancy has tremendous knowledge to contribute to the moms of special needs children. She has navigated through hospital, educational, and government systems, serving as Amanda's unwavering advocate for more than 21 years. She is a wealth of knowledge and has a vast amount of knowledge about resources most parents of special needs children don't even know exist.

Like most women, after Lyndsay headed off to college—and ultimately to her new life in New York—Nancy started cleaning up some of the day-in-and-day-out things around her.

She spent a year focusing on her home and space—new roof, new siding, new windows, new stone patio, new landscaping, interior redecorating, and decluttering. This nest is ready for her next two decades. And she's been giving attention to her joy, calmness and spirituality as a way to manage anxiety that she experiences in her daily life. I love seeing her progress in this area because it contributes to her happiness and confidence. Over the past couple of years, she has also made adjustments in her food choices, mentored in this area by her daughter, Lyndsay.

Yes, Nancy is on the bridge, moving toward a better version of her already-amazing self.

Along with the things Nancy has given attention to above—on the operations side of life—she also sees Amanda settling into a better place in her own life. Things feel calmer and more settled at home.

Now, Nancy is thinking about a new purpose in her life. It's something that has been percolating within her for a long time, waiting for the time to be right.

She's ready to help moms of special needs daughters. Of course, she doesn't have all the answers, but she does have a starting point.

Here is what she knows:

- She would like to help Christian women, because she knows she wants an element of faith and prayer woven into the process.
- She would like to help women who have daughters, because that's what she knows best.
- She would like to help women whose daughters are between 18 and 25. Nancy explained it this way, "These are difficult years, because these kids age out of a lot of the resources that are provided by the government and by schools." This is also what Nancy is living through right now, so she is current on the issues.
- She would like to start with a small group of women to get started.
- And, finally, she knows her next best step is to start talking about this with some of the people she knows helping those in the autism and special needs community. Nancy believes she will be able to bring in her first group of members through word-of-mouth conversations.

I love so many things about Nancy's approach to get started:

- Nancy is on fire about this.
- Moms are going to have the support of a guide who has done the hard work to discover the resources.
- Nancy's journey with Amanda will serve a God-given purpose. Nancy has always known that God hand-picked her to be Amanda's mom.

Nancy is on the bridge. She is moving through her success path.

Success path? "Wait!" You ask, "What's that?"

Yes, I'm introducing you to a new idea: The Success Path. Rather than viewing our journey across the bridge as one homogenous trip, let's look at your journey in six stages.

This success path is designed to help you get a strong start and to help you know where you're going—even when your destination seems too far away. Every journey happens one step at a time. Most of the time, the only thing you need to know is the next step ahead of you.

Before we get on the bridge, however, let's come up with a plan that will serve as your road map so you know every step is in the right direction. You might want to start by reviewing your checklist from Chapter 3. It provides an overview of the things you are struggling to overcome. Your struggles may be mild, moderate, or full-on challenging. Everyone starts in Stage Zero.

Now, with the struggles you face fresh in mind, let's get started and map out *your* journey!

## Stage One: Assess Your Life

In this stage, you are declaring that you're ready to make progress in your life. You want more. Your first step is to assess your current levels of satisfaction in ten areas of your life. You took a good look at these ten areas in Chapter 4: *Clean Up the Things That Matter To You.* Perhaps you paused to complete the Women Who Spark Life Assessment. If you haven't done that yet, this is the perfect time to do it. When you've completed the assessment, you will have completed Stage One. You can find it at www.aletanorris.com/life-assessment.

This stage is important. You need to get a handle on what's in front of and around you. You don't want to be stepping over and around an unexpected pile of struggle on your journey across the bridge. Before I wrote my first *Women Who Spark* book, I got ready for it. The priority I uncovered when I looked around and assessed my day-in-and-day-out life was to declutter the house from top to bottom. You may recall, before that, my big, huge, gargantuan clean up was my finances.

Nancy completed the Women Who Spark Life Assessment and uncovered *Spirituality, Joy, Peace, and Contentment* as her area to clean up. Clean up may not be the word she would use on her journey, but she sure brightened her life by tackling this area. Identifying this as her area of focus allowed her to move on to Stage Two.

As you complete the life assessment, you will identify three areas that you feel need attention. Before we move on, where are you?

- ☐ Wow, I've completed Stage One. Woo hoo! I've done the life assessment and have identified three areas that need attention.

- ☐ Not there yet. I'm thinking about it, and as soon as I free up some time and space for this, I'm on it. Life Assessment, here I come!

## Stage Two: Create Your Initial Plan

You're on to Stage Two after you've completed the Women Who Spark Life Assessment and identify your three areas to work on. In Stage Two, you will create a plan for only one of those areas. Yes, just one. I know, the temptation to dive in with all three will be intense and it may be difficult to decide which one to choose.

However, focusing on one area is important. This is all about setting yourself up for success. If you take on too much at one time, you set yourself up for a greater likelihood of failing.

**If you take on too much at one time, you set yourself up for a greater likelihood of failing.**

I want to focus on this one area: ______________

______________________________

Creating your plan will start with brainstorming all the things you *could* do related to this area of your life. Here's what Nancy said:

> My area of focus is growing my faith and tending more intentionally to the spiritual part of my life. A few of my brainstorm ideas that I will start with are to develop a plan to read the bible in bite-size pieces—Yes! The whole thing! I have read parts many times, and I want to do this. Also, I will start a daily gratitude journal, and I will improve *how*

I pray. I came up with about 20 ideas, and these are the ones I will start with.

This is perfect! Nancy has a plan that is manageable and meaningful. She is setting herself up for success by not taking on too much. She is currently researching resources for her bible-reading goal. When you're not sure how to move forward with an idea, it can paralyze you. Research! That is always your first step when you're stuck.

Research will differ from person to person. You can talk to people, buy books, use your search engines, or jump on YouTube. Feel comfortable doing what suits you best.

In Stage Two, you are making your initial progress across the bridge by making progress in one area of your life. You are likely feeling better about yourself, even happier. Progress does that.

Before we move on, where are you?

- ☐ Yep, I've got Stage Two covered. I'm focusing on one area, and I've brainstormed the things I'm doing to improve in this area.
- ☐ No, not there yet, but it won't be long. As soon as I decide which area to begin with, the brainstorming will begin.

Now, let's see what happens in Stage Three.

## Stage Three: Turn Your Progress Into Joy

Too many women show up in the world looking for joy.

No, no, no. Don't expect the joy, BRING the joy! Cultivate joy. Manufacture joy.

As you continue to make progress in your first area of focus, I want you to begin thinking about your second area. Is it your finances? Or your health and fitness?

Nancy had a head start when she began working on the spiritual part of her life. Remember she had spent a year with an intense focus on her home and space. During that time, she also started thinking more carefully about her food choices. Her focus on the spiritual part of her life is theoretically the third area she's focusing on.

And do you know what's happening? Nancy has more joy. She feels happier, calmer, and less anxious. This is a lot of progress from where she was at six years ago, immediately following her divorce.

In Stage Three, Nancy is experiencing a sense of joy, because she is making progress in her life—in multiple areas. That's the essence of Stage Three. You are now focusing on three or more areas of your life. You are making progress, and things are feeling more settled. You're in control of things that fell by the way before.

Perhaps, like Nancy, you've been working on some areas of your life prior to reading this book. If so, you may have a head start. Or, like many women, you may be starting at ground zero.

It's possible you'll stay in Stage Three for several months—or even several years.

I spent a decade getting my financial situation back on solid ground. During those years, I was deeply rooted in the messy middle of my life: divorce recovery, raising my kids, investing for their college, paying the mortgage, running a business with Nancy, squeezing in workouts, keeping the house in a reasonable state of repair, and trying to get six hours of sleep. My deepest Stage Zero was in 2004, the day I walked out of court following my second divorce. My list of struggles was long. But, thankfully, I stepped onto the bridge. I started to make progress.

I was still in Stage Three when I met my current husband in 2010—and would be for about six more years. When you learn about Stages Four through Six, you will see that you could choose to stay in Stage Three forever. For some women, it will be the perfect place to be: working on the day-in-and-day-out areas of their lives and choosing to not settle for less than they could.

So, don't be discouraged by long timelines. If we keep a long-term perspective, doing deep work in our life over several years makes a lot of sense. In 2004, I was 41 years old. If I'm living into my 80s, it does not seem so daunting to be *actively* doing the work to improve the level of happiness, confidence and sense of purpose I will feel in ten areas of my life for decades to come.

**Whether you choose to do the work or not, the time will still pass. I don't want you ten years into the future and still stuck in the same place dissatisfied and struggling.**

Stage Three can be looked at as simply making yourself a priority in your life. Whether you choose to do the work or not, the time will still pass. I don't want you ten years into the future and still stuck in the same place dissatisfied and struggling.

If we could stay in Stage Three forever, then why move onto another stage?

Stages Four and Five have more to do with the runway than the bridge. They involve jetting off into a new vision or dream for your future life, really leaning into what's possible for your 80-year-old self.

You can decide, after you've taken a look at the next two stages, if your new land is so far away, it may require some airline travel ... or if you're perfectly content to get to your new land on foot.

Where are you?

- ☐ I'm on my way to settling into Stage Three. I can see I have things to work on and progress to make.
- ☐ I'm not here yet. I'm still working on one priority back in Stage Two and comfortable to hang out there for a while.
- ☐ I'm killin' it in three or more areas of focus. I've got a dream percolating within me, so on to Stage Four I go!

## Stage Four: Investigate Your Future Dreams

When you begin to explore your dreams, you are venturing into the unknown and imagining possibilities. In Stage Four, you are actively dreaming about a future vision. You've reignited your day-to-day life in Stages One through Three. You're feeling better about your current state of life. Now, you have the capacity to imagine there could be more. You are ready to actually reinvent yourself.

What is on your wish list? What has been whispering to you for years? What are other women doing that you want to be doing? What has eluded you for years while you've been busy with the messy middle? What do you want that you feel you can't achieve—yet?

For Nancy, it's her new vision helping moms with special needs daughters. While Nancy would have been an amazing resource for moms years ago—given all the research, advocating, and navigating she has done for 21 years—she wasn't ready.

As I shared, Nancy had a lot of messy middle. She was immersed in keeping her house, family, and business afloat for the past 25 years.

Now, she is making progress. Things have settled down a bit around her. She's found her joy again, and now she's ready for a passion project. She is investigating this future dream.

In Stage Four, you recognize that there *is* a dream. And you dare to image that you deserve it and that you can achieve it.

Nancy's dream came to her easily. She knows what it is, so she won't hang out in Stage Four for long. I also knew my dream. It was to write a book to help women navigate through the messy middle of life. I uncovered that dream in 2006 when I hired my coach, Katie Brazelton, to help me craft my life plan.

I hung out in Stage Four for more than a decade before I moved on to Stage Five. For me, Stage Four overlapped my work in Stages Two and Three. While I was busy shoring up some things in my day-to-day life, I had investigated and identified a dream to pursue in the future.

You can see the difference between me and Nancy. My dream became clear to me a decade before I was ready to act on it. Nancy's dream is emerging now, and she is ready to move on to Step Five to put a strategy in place.

I have one more Stage Four scenario. My friend, Lori, mentioned briefly in Chapter 1, has had a 30-year-long career. She dreams of doing something completely different in her professional career. She doesn't know what that will be. She is giving herself one year to investigate options and possibilities. She will be actively working in her Stage Four for several months.

Remember, when you don't know *how,* you can start with research. That also works if you don't know *what.*

Where are you?

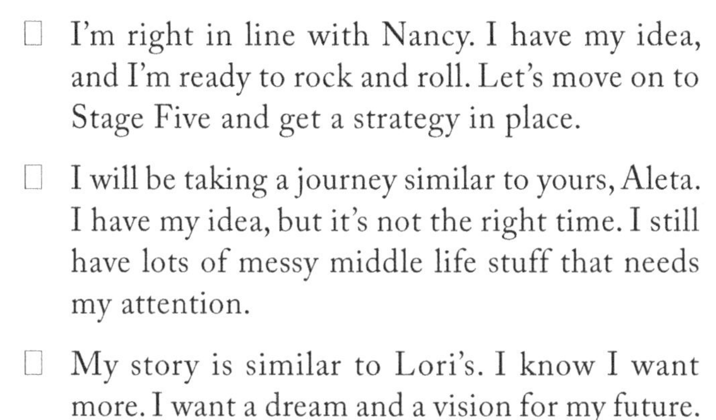

- ☐ I'm right in line with Nancy. I have my idea, and I'm ready to rock and roll. Let's move on to Stage Five and get a strategy in place.
- ☐ I will be taking a journey similar to yours, Aleta. I have my idea, but it's not the right time. I still have lots of messy middle life stuff that needs my attention.
- ☐ My story is similar to Lori's. I know I want more. I want a dream and a vision for my future. I don't know what it is yet, so I'll be doing some exploring.

When you are clear about your future dreams, it's time to create a strategy, so on to Stage Five we go.

## Stage Five: Organize Your Strategy

I love this stage. How can you not be excited?

You have a dream, and now you're going to figure out how to move toward that dream. If you look at the example list below, it is likely evident to you that you won't accomplish any of these with a simple to-do list.

- You'd like to start a new business.
- You want to advance a passion project like Nancy is doing.

- You have a hobby you'd like to monetize.
- You want to sell your house and move to a new place in the country—or even the world.
- You'd like to start an online marketing busines.
- You're ready to discover a new career.
- It's time for you to overhaul health and fitness.

These kinds of dreams and visions require strategy. This is where we start to dig deep. What is involved in your reinvention?

This is where Nancy is right now. She identified her passion project in Stage Four, and now she is beginning to put her strategy in place.

I identified my passion project in 2006 (Stage Four), and I began putting my Women Who Spark strategy in place in August of 2017 (Stage Five). That is when I began writing *Women Who Spark: 12 Steps to Catapult Happiness, Cultivate Confidence, and Discover the Purpose of Your Life.* While I was writing, I began drafting the strategy for an online course, starting a Facebook Community, designing keynote addresses, and planning how to market and release the book.

Where are you at?

- ☐ I'm ready to dive into my strategy for the dreams and vision I have for my future. Let's go!
- ☐ I'm not here yet, but I'm sure getting excited about when that day arrives.

As we move into the next section of the book, we're preparing for action. I'll provide the framework for putting a master strategy in place. Before you roll up your sleeves and think about creating your master strategy, which we'll explore in Chapter 15, there are a few more things we need to take a look at. So, sit tight.

Meanwhile, we'll wrap up by sharing the insights for Stage Six.

## Stage Six: Navigate Toward Your Amazing Future Self

This stage is exactly what the title suggests. You are continuing to navigate toward your amazing future self. You are not settling for "good enough" in your life. And you are certainly not settling for "less than."

You may continue to navigate forward—across the bridge—by focusing on the operations side of your life: the ten areas of life that we've been talking about. This is where you will find happiness and confidence. It is also where you will serve your purpose.

Or you may be jetting across the runway, taking off to bigger dreams and visions for where you will go with your life, who you will be, and how you will make a difference in the world.

Stage Six doesn't end. At least not if you're committed to living an amazing life through the second half.

The Success Path will be a constant companion in your life, especially if you are committed to making progress.

Where are you at?

- ☐ I get it. I see Stage Six as an ongoing part of the journey. Consider me there.
- ☐ No, I'm feeling overwhelmed!

This is a lot.

If you're feeling overwhelmed by the thought of this progress, I get it. It's not uncommon. This is why I created a membership community called "Accountability and Friendship for Success." This is a community for women who know they want more and who also recognize they'll do better—and make more progress—if they have some structure for accountability in community with other like-minded women.

In this membership, I help women in midlife who feel restless and unsure what's next reignite and reinvent their lives for greater happiness, confidence, accomplishment, and clarity of purpose. You can learn more at www.aletanorris.com/AFSMembership.

## Let's Get Real About the Tough Stuff

I can't think of a better way to recap this chapter than to end with an acknowledgement of everything Nancy went through to get where she's at today.

Since I first drafted this chapter, Nancy has made progress getting her passion project off the ground. I can already tell her influence and impact in the special needs community will be significant. She has captured the attention of other leaders in this community who have recognized the "diamond in the rough" that Nancy is.

She has been invited to be on a non-profit board, and was told, "We have big plans for you!"

But the passion project didn't happen overnight, and it didn't come easy.

For 21 years, aside from taking care of her family (as most moms do) and running a business (as some women do), Nancy has been the primary caretaker and advocate for Amanda. It has been an all-consuming responsibility.

Along the way, I've seen Nancy circling in Stages Two and Three—as we all do—doing the best she can to manage the day-to-day responsibilities of her life.

1. She tried to be the best **mom** to her two daughters that she could be.
2. She gave steady attention to the care and upkeep of her **home and space.**
3. She was committed to her **career.**
4. She tried to find the time and have a plan to take care of her **health and fitness.**
5. She made conscious efforts to nurture **friendships** within the context of a difficult schedule. After all, how many women are still finding "caregivers" for their 21-year-old daughters so they can meet friends for a glass of wine?
6. She was fully responsible for her **finances** as a single-parent household.
7. She tried to find time to incorporate practices for **joy, peace, and contentment**, more recently returning to a strong faith life that was once a cornerstone in her life.
8. She hasn't exactly had time for **hobbies and interests**, but I know Nancy has enjoyed her work and her role as a mom.
9. She's made her extended **family** a priority along the way and is always available when needed.

Yes, it's true. Nancy has been acutely busy in Stages Two and Three for 21 years. More than that, actually. And now, it's time.

It's time for her to do something she feels passionate about. It's exciting to be on the sidelines watching her discover something she knows will make a difference in the world.

What's the lesson in all of this for you? Time. There is time. Your passion projects and your bigger life purpose will be revealed to you when the time is right.

**Chapter Highlights**

**Chapter 1: Is There More to Life Than This?**

- Get clear about what is nagging at you, feels unresolved, and needs your attention.

**Chapter 2: Let's Get a Few Things Straight**

- You have a runway ahead of you for the second half of your life and can change your beliefs about what lies ahead.

**Chapter 3: The Sparks Have Dimmed**

- Many mid-life women experience apathy. You can treasure the memories in your positive bucket and do the work to leave the negative bucket of memories behind.

**Chapter 4: Clean Up the Things That Matter to You**

- When you look around, what do you notice? As you assess ten areas of your life, what areas need to be cleaned up? Which need to be reignited and reinvented?

**Chapter 5: Women Who Took Action to Clean Up the Mess**

- A bridge connects the old land to the new land. You don't have to have a clear picture of your new land to step onto the bridge.

**Chapter 6: It's Time to Reignite and Reinvent**

- You may very well have three, four or five decades left, and you have a choice to settle for where you're at, reignite or reinvent.

**Chapter 7: Design Your 80-Year Old Self**

- Envision a lovely woman you know who is in her 80s, and think about your own 80-year-old self.

**Chapter 8: Inspiration From Women in Their 70s, 80s, and 90s**

- You can be fully alive in the later years of your life.

**Chapter 9: Believe in Yourself**

- Belief precedes action, your belief in yourself is determined by you.

**Chapter 10: Transform Yourself for Action**

- Acknowledge that you have time and create a vision for your future. Then, get ready.

**Chapter 11: Get Started. Where Are YOU Going?**

- Stage One: Assess Your Life
- Stage Two: Create Your Initial Plan
- Stage Three: Turn Your Progress Into Joy
- Stage Four: Investigate Your Future Dreams
- Stage Five: Organize Your Strategy
- Stage Six: Navigate Toward Your Amazing Future Self

# CHAPTER 12

## Women Who Are Doing It

*Life isn't about finding yourself.*
*Life is about creating yourself.*

~ George Bernard Shaw

After 25 years in a successful, direct-selling career, a middle-aged grandmother felt called to a challenge. Following her retirement, she wanted to be useful. Not entirely certain what that would be, she decided to write a management training book, one where she could share all of the factors that would create a "dream company," one where women would be allowed to achieve unlimited possibilities. In the process of writing her book, she asked herself,

"Why are you theorizing about a dream company?
Why don't you just start one?"

On September 13, 1963, Mary Kay Ash founded Mary Kay Cosmetics.[8]

At the time of her death in 2001—38 years later—Mary Kay Ash had amassed a personal fortune of $98 million. Her company had more than $1.2 billion in sales and an international sales force of more than eight hundred thousand women in at least three dozen countries.

She started her company when she was 45 years old, right at the cusp of our official definition of *middle age*. Remember, we may have two, three, or four decades ahead of us. That time represents an incredible amount of potential. Mary Kay Ash grasped the opportunity to remain productive and contribute even more to the world following a successful career. She not only started a "dream company," but also led its growth for almost 40 years.

I am so inspired by this story. Did you do the math? Mary Kay's formal professional career lasted for 25 years. Her dream career lasted for 38 years.

It's never too late to discover new dreams and lead an incredible life.

In the remainder of this chapter, you will meet women who reignited or reinvented their lives for the second half. I hope you have as much fun reading this chapter as I had creating it.

As I spent hours interviewing these incredible women, I found myself becoming more excited about my own future potential.

Prepare to be inspired—and envision telling your own story someday.

Don't get stuck thinking, "I wish I could do something like that, but I'm not her." If you pay attention, you will notice each woman's story varies by degree. The journeys are personal and each woman is sharing what made a difference in her life.

But there are some common elements to look for and apply to your own life.

As you read each story ask yourself these questions:

- What could I do to get my spark back like that?
- Do I have an unrealized dream like she did?
- How can I rediscover my confidence?
- Is there a way I can find greater happiness?
- What can be the trigger for unleashing my undiscovered purpose?

Each of these stories represents happiness, confidence, and sense of purpose for the woman telling the story.

Let's get started!

## Cathy Studer, Age 54

*A survivor of childhood sexual abuse; became an author at age 50 to help other women heal.*

Cathy Studer had a lifelong career as a hairstylist. She was content with her job and had no intention of doing anything different. She loved helping people feel better about themselves by looking better.

Then one day a conversation with one of her longtime clients became the catalyst to ultimately take her on a journey of vulnerability and courage. Cathy says,

"Little did I know I would add a new path for a purpose in my life in my 50s!"

But that's exactly what happened when she had a deep conversation with a customer. After a client first shared her childhood abuse story, Cathy shared her own, which she had never done before. They bonded in empathy with similar trauma experiences. During her next appointment, her client asked Cathy if she had suffered from depression or PTSD, as the client was suffering from both. After pausing, Cathy replied, "I had tremendous shame, humiliation, low self-worth, and very low self-esteem; however, I did not suffer from depression or PTSD. Don't get me wrong, I was broken and had a journey to heal."

Her client looked her right in the eye and said, "You need to write a book, girlfriend!" The spark she never saw coming was now lit. After reflection, deep introspection, and prayer, Cathy stepped into that mission. It took courage as she faced the fear of letting the world hear her story.

She is now the author of a self-help book called *Broken to Beautifully Whole.* In her book, she delves into why some people who suffer childhood trauma can overcome and experience success while others struggle and suffer. Cathy shared, "I did not have depression or PTSD, but I have struggled with extreme shame and lack of trust in humanity. In my book, I share the six compelling attributes that I used in my healing pilgrimage that pulled my broken pieces back together while reducing my chances for depression or PTSD."

She speaks to groups to share how the journey from brokenness to wholeness is truly possible as you can become "Kintsugi"! (If you've never seen Japanese Kintsugi pottery—an ancient and beautiful repair technique—be sure to look it up online!)

This second career is incredibly meaningful for Cathy, "For the first time in my life, I am comfortable sharing my story, and I know I am meant to take this journey. I feel so empowered because I have truly found my purpose.'"

You can connect with Cathy at www.cathystuder.com and on Facebook at @brokentobeautifullywhole.

## Terry Fulcher, Age 65

*Went back to grad school at age 50, then later started her own consulting business at age 61.*

Terry Fulcher inspired women in her peer group to go back to college in their 50s. How did she do it? By doing it first. It all started when she felt a call in her life to lead her team more effectively for the work she was doing. So, at age 50, she went back to school to earn her master's degree. That equipped her to move up in her organization where she enjoyed a fulfilling career until, at age 61, she formed her own LLC consulting business. And now, four years later, she still feels like she is just getting started.

During my interview with Terry, I was struck by how lovely she is. Calm, kind, poised, and simply at ease all around. One could assume while listening to Terry that she has been blessed with a productive, smooth life, one that came to fruition nicely.

I asked her, "Have you experienced a messy middle in your life?" Instantly, she said, "Yes!" She explained that her daughter had given birth to a baby at age 15, a baby she chose to give up for adoption. This sounds like a moment that would be difficult for a mom, yes? It definitely qualifies as a messy-middle moment.

Then, a year later, her daughter gave birth to another baby. This time, Terry and her husband made the decision to assist in raising the baby, providing interim foster care and ongoing support for their daughter while she grew into her parenting responsibilities.

The story has a happy ending. Terry's daughter has made a good life for her and her daughter—and Terry has a beautiful granddaughter. Thankfully, difficult life situations don't always remain difficult.

You can connect with Terry at https://resource-full.com.

## Laurie Hanson, Age 56

*Left corporate America and started a home-based yoga business at age 50 then another business at age 55*

It wasn't until someone posed a question to Laurie five years into her marriage that she started to pay closer attention: "Why do you always do everything he tells you to do?"

The way Laurie saw it, she was being a dutiful wife. After all, her dreams were all coming true, exactly as she envisioned while she was in college. She had launched a successful retail career and was managing an upscale store in a large city, she was happily married, and living in the big house of her dreams.

Over the next couple of years, however, some things began to bother Laurie. She and her husband were not seeing eye to eye on when to start their family, and Laurie made another discovery that she later learned was, to her, an unforgivable issue. Still, they forged ahead, trying to make a go of it as a family.

Like many couples, they began navigating through marriage struggles. And after their first (and only) child was born, they made the decision to move back to Laurie's hometown for a fresh start. It seemed surreal to Laurie that in a short time, she went from being on top of the world, loving her career, feeling eager to start a family and enjoying a high level of confidence ... to feeling shattered. By the time they had moved, the survival of her marriage was in question, she had taken a big step back in her career, and her confidence was shattered. The beautiful light in her life was her new daughter.

Laurie's marriage ended when her daughter was two years old, and she was officially in the messy middle of life. Her sparks had dimmed. I asked Laurie what she did to find her spark again.

> I began to work on my career and soon settled into a new role, one that would prove to be a stepping-stone to a bigger opportunity. I was struggling, though, because I was renting a flat in a duplex, and this did not match my dream in any way. It was the day I bought my first house by myself that I could really feel my confidence and spark coming back. Over the years, I loved doing home improvement projects and working in my yard. I learned a lot and really enjoyed my independence.
>
> Step by step, one step at a time, I rebuilt my life. Meeting my now-husband has been an amazing blessing and something I was really looking forward to—being married again. I know that is not what every woman is looking for, but it was very important to me. We're very happily married. Two years ago, I was laid off from my big job, and it became a great opportunity for me to reinvent

> my life, again. I earned my yoga certification and started a second home-based business. I now operate more from a heart-centered place.
>
> I am settling into my life in my mid-50s and have my heart set on doing work that makes me happy. I'm done with the big jobs that keep me awake at night. I have a lot of years ahead of me, and I want to dedicate them to helping people.

You can connect with Laurie at heartcenteryogalife.com or at ljhanson.myrandf.com.

## Mandy Hinerman, Age 64

*After experiencing difficult marriages and a variety of careers over more than four decades, Mandy is still planning to return to her unfulfilled dream of being an artist.*

Mandy knew before she even walked down the aisle as a 19-year-old bride that she was making a mistake. The verbal abuse was already there and signs of future physical abuse lingered in the air.

The messy middle began early for Mandy—before her 20th birthday—and would last for more than 25 years. By the time she got married, she had already given up her only dream: going to art school.

After 25 years, three kids, and lot of confidence-busting verbal abuse from her philandering husband, one of Mandy's dearest friends gave her some tough love advice: "Do something. I love you, and you're my friend, but I cannot keep hearing you tell me these stories of hardship then see you do nothing about it."

But Mandy believed her husband when he said:

- *You bring nothing to the table.*
- *You'll never leave.*
- *How can you support yourself?*
- *I'll make sure you never see the kids. I'll tell them you're crazy.*

Finally, one day, inspired by what she noticed about her aunt and uncle's miserable marriage, she envisioned a future in her 80s that would look the same. It was the catalyst for action.

Mandy eventually made the leap from her bad marriage. That was already 20 years ago. Because she is incredibly sparkly today, I asked her how she got her spark back.

> It started to come back immediately! As soon as the weight of emotional abuse was lifted, my physical health improved. And, I started to do things, one by one. I bought a house; I began finding work in my field of interior design to boost my income, and my reputation in my field began to strengthen. I've done things in my career I never thought possible. The Spark came from realizing I *could* do these things. With everything I did, more of my confidence came back. Leaving that marriage was the most freeing thing I've ever done. I had to take a deep breath and jump.

It's been 20 years since Mandy left her difficult 25-year-long marriage. She has been married to a wonderful man for 15 years and has enough time on the horizon to have an even longer-than-25-year marriage that is happy, positive, and affirming.

Mandy's mother is 96 years old, still a vibrant member of their family and a mentor to her grandchildren.

I asked Mandy what she will do with the next thirty years of her life. "I'll continue working for several more years, because I love what I do. And my art. I will get back to my dream of pursuing my art."

Remember the idea I shared earlier about living our lives in 20-year increments? I love Mandy's story, because that is exactly what she's done. The first 20 years were spent growing up—with a childhood that was, in her words, stifling. Twenty-five years of a difficult marriage. Fifteen years with her current husband. And 30 more years ahead of her—if she is as blessed with the same level of good health her mom enjoys.

At age 64, she is still dreaming about what's next.

Mandy's life is proof you don't ever have to think your life is defined by a couple of bad decades.

## Christine Bukowski, Age 60

*Reinvented herself from professional fundraiser to urban schoolteacher to college professor*

"If we're in a place where we don't feel valued, it's time to go find a place where we are valued," Christine told me.

Raised with what she refers to as a lot of privilege, Christine was always mindful of giving back to the community. She spent the first fifteen years of her career involved in professional fundraising.

At one point, she stepped back and asked herself, "What kind of a difference am I really making in the community if I'm raising funds for the symphony?" She was quick to add, "The arts are important; I simply didn't know if that's where I wanted to be of service."

In 2003, Christine—who was in her 40s—came upon a program to get her teaching certificate and master's degree to teach in an urban school. She said,

> This had always been in the back of my mind as something I had wanted to do. This program opened my mind to a lot of things.
>
> It was very challenging to be teaching in an urban school and going to school, raising a family ... all these things happening at the same time. All these things were important.
>
> At school, I had so many other things to deal with. It wasn't just about math and science. Relationships—the ones teachers had with students—were so important. The students needed to trust us. We were working with a high trauma population: poverty, single-parent households, food insecurity, and homelessness.
>
> After 15 years in the urban classroom—and education in general—so much had changed. Teachers were being asked to do more and more and not being given resources. Many things were heartbreaking to see. In 2018, I decided, given the daily things that were involved in running a classroom without the support of administration, it was time for me to step back from the classroom role.

I asked her, "Did you ever lose your spark along the way?"

> Sure! There was a time I had stepped back from doing non-profit work full time—the kids were

> in grade school and middle school—it was a lot to juggle. I was doing consulting work in the fund-raising space with an organization that our family was very involved in. At one point, they told me my services were no longer needed. It was devastating. I had to handle it well because my kids were still involved in the organization. I did not want to have their experiences with the organization clouded by my feelings of betrayal by that organization.
>
> I had gone above and beyond, and they had not seen my value. I was fired from a job I felt was my dream job. It was hard to crawl out of that, but I was determined that I couldn't let that organization determine what is important to a family. A job loss is significant and it took a toll. I really needed to rethink what I want to do. That was the point when I decided to go back to school to become a teacher.

It was apparent to Christine that even her most difficult season had a silver lining. She told me it was apparent her first day as a teacher, "I was in the classroom writing my name on the board with the date, and I knew that is where I was supposed to be."

Fifteen years later, Christine decided it was time to bring the classroom teaching chapter to a close. It was time to chase after a new dream.

It turned out, she would have a fairly soft landing.

Christine and her husband were enjoying a weekend get-away in lovely Door County, Wisconsin. They befriended another couple during a bread-baking class. While making and eating a variety of breads, Christine's new friend shared that she had worked her whole life in

Chicago in advertising. Now, at age 70, she was teaching at Loyola University in Chicago. That sparked an idea for Christine.

She went back to her alma mater to see what opportunities might exist. "I talked to the Dean at Alverno College." Christine said, "I understood the culture there, the Franciscan values, the unique values of each person, fostering peace and justice. I knew Alverno was a feminist environment. The nuns were still in the classroom teaching into their 80s. Agism was not going to be an issue, and my being in my 50s would not be an issue in any way."

The dean came back with an offer. "We want you to teach our teachers."

It was perfect! Christine began teaching a program for paraprofessionals, individuals who would finish their degrees and then get their teaching degrees. Then, in the spring of that year, she was asked to teach a new course over 12 weeks.

Now having entered her 60s, Christine is grateful for this new career. She wrapped up our conversation saying, "As I've gotten older, I am concerned about how I value myself and less concerned about how others value me."

## Debbie Norris, Age 51

*Unable to have children, battled cancer, and lost a bonus daughter to cancer. Debbie is now active in the ovarian cancer community and finding joy in her hobbies.*

Debbie has experienced more than her share of sadness and emotional pain.

She told me, "When I was 43, I was diagnosed with ovarian cancer. Two years later my youngest bonus daughter was diagnosed with childhood cancer, and 22 months later she passed away."

As if this were not enough of a test, in October of 2019, Debbie was let go from a job she had held for eight and a half years. She was a top performer in the department.

She said, "The depression I was already experiencing from all the previous mess intensified and I spiraled down deep. I started working with a wonderful Christian counselor, and eventually got a new position in childcare on Dec 31, 2019."

At the same time, Debbie started to focus more on her hobbies: photography and crochet. She started doing more photo sessions and selling at craft fairs.

> I now am back doing work I love every day—making a difference in the lives of babies and their parents—and enjoying my hobbies. I'm also writing a blog on my experiences through cancer, grief, and not being able to have children of my own. I've regained confidence, happiness, and sense of purpose.

Debbie is also active in the ovarian cancer community, along with her husband, presenting their story to medical students, locally, and sharing their story as a survivor and caregiver, nationally.

You can read Debbie's blog—which is beautiful—at bornwithamothersheart.blogspot.com.

## Angela Smith, Age 56,

*Following careers as a teacher, stay-at-home-mom, and a CNA, Angela is now a published author and has started a new career on the sales team of her publishing company. She is also starting her own company to help women use art to support their healing process.*

When Angela became an empty nester at age 50, she was tired of taking care of everyone but herself. She knew in order to move toward her destiny beyond motherhood she would have to concentrate on the whole self—mind, body, and soul. It was time to dig deep to nurture the messy parts of her heart, to be able to continue serving others in a healthy way.

At the time of her divorce two years earlier, Angela was the mother of three children (one severely disabled) and had been out of the workforce for 22 years. She said,

> I was facing a scary world of getting back into the work force with outdated skills as a former teacher and burnout from being a CNA. I was tired of taking care of everyone else. When I became an empty nester at the age of 50, I knew it was time to take care of me!

One of the first things Angela did was join Author Academy Elite to finish her book, *Voiceless—Spencer's Story: A Mother's Journey Raising a Son with Significant Needs.* She told me,

> It was one of the best decisions of my life! Writing the book helped my healing process, as well as painting, pottery, making jewelry, and traveling.

Since the launch of her book in 2016 (when she was 52), Angela has worked in dementia care, done secretarial work at a chiropractors office, taught English as a Second Language to kids in China, moved three times, been on a mission trip to El Salvador, and gotten remarried.

Now in her mid-fifties, Angela was recently hired for the sales team for Author Academy Elite. She is passionate about helping other people get their stories out to the world. Angela is also looking at starting her own business. She told me, "I want to encourage women to engage in an art form to help with their healing process so they can pursue their purpose with passion."

Angela's book, *"Voiceless—Spencer's Story: A Mother's Journey Raising a Son with Significant Needs"* is available on Amazon.

You can find Angela at www.angeladee.life and on Instagram at author.angela.

## Donna Cowan, Age 59

*After 25 years fighting a debilitating illness and enduring 59 surgeries, Donna became a children's book author at age 58.*

Donna says, "My youngest granddaughter, plus my other grands, had a hand in encouraging me to chase after my dusty dreams. They are amazed and thrilled to learn that even at my age, dreams can come true."

She grew up in a large family in Oklahoma. A shy, introverted child—and the youngest in the family—Donna taught herself to read before she was five years old.

She said, "I often ran out of things to read, so I started making up my own stories. I'd write them down and act them out. I played by myself a lot."

Her author career was sidetracked by a series of severe life difficulties.

Into her adult life, after a string of bad marriages, Donna was 37 years old when she married her current husband. "Right before I met him," she told me, "I was diagnosed with a neuro-muscular disease. It stopped me in my tracks. There was no real treatment or therapy for it. I stopped working, and in the last 25 years, I've had 59 surgeries!"

"My husband has been with me every step of the way," Donna said. "In 2015, I had five surgeries, and when I was recovering, my husband said, 'It is time you stop putting off your dream and go for it.'"

Were it not for her husband's encouragement, Donna would not be a children's book author today. One of the perks?

> It draws me so much closer to my grandchildren. I love each and every one of them. My book was inspired by my youngest granddaughter when I was talking with her about my cats.
>
> She asked what I thought my cats did all night when they went outside. I didn't know what to tell her, so I told her the cat was a superhero going out at night saving her animal friends. All of my grandchildren loved the story and had me tell it to them all of the time.
>
> When I needed a backstory for the books, I invented superhero school.

Donna published her first children's book at age 58 and her second title a year later.

What's next for Donna? She shared,

> I live life as fully as possible. I am eager to learn and share the journey with my fellow travelers, whether just beginning, on the way, or at the peak of commitment. We all stumble and fail, but learn that getting up again is the biggest reward.
>
> We all need to stop waiting for that "magical" permission slip to appear in our lives. The truth is, no one knows what is inside you until you are ready to let it shine through. Blaze on.
>
> I have learned so much and expanded my circle of friends and relationships. I feel inspired every day because I know someone, somewhere needs my encouragement, my help, my belief in them. Sparking a tiny flame is stupendous! Seeing the light click on and the mind whirl with possibilities is priceless. My new job is awesome! I get to make things up for a living...who else can say that?

Donna also has more on her mind than writing books.

> I now go into schools and help kids build their self-esteem. They have a superhero within them, and they can find it. It may be as simple as being a good friend or helping someone who needs help. Do they want to become an author or a writer? I'd like to help them do some writing. I am now developing a 'learn to write a story' program for schools.

I asked Donna what has inspired her about all of this newfound activity in her life.

> It's surprised me that I've been able to do this. I had kind of given up. I told myself, 'This is my life now. I'm never going to do anything important because my life is such a bad thing.' Also, it's opened up an entire world to me to help other people who aren't clear. I do 20 calls a week helping someone with what they want to write. I also do some editing work through the guild at Author Academy Elite, and I'm one of the author liaisons for AAE, helping people who are stuck somewhere in the program. I am also on the children's author advisory team and will likely take over as the coach."
>
> My original plan was:
>
> - Get the book done.
> - Sell the book.
> - Get it into schools.
> - Speak here and there.

What has happened is that the book has gotten smaller and everything else around it has gotten bigger. Doors have opened for me that I never would have imagined.

Intrigued to learn more about Donna's Superhero School Series? You can find her books on Amazon: *With the Courage of a Mouse* and *With the Curiosity of a Cat.* Keep your eyes open for *With the Passion of a Pig.* You can connect with Donna at donnacowanauthor@gmail.com.

## Audrey Jett, Age 52

*Patiently waited through her 40s and into her 50s to discover her Spark.*

"I had been preparing and waiting and hoping for things to happen in my 40s that just didn't happen," Audrey told me.

Audrey Jett knew, however, that things would evolve in her life in God's time.

It was in her 50s that things started to take shape for Audrey, who has worked in the financial services industry for more than three decades.

A few years earlier, she had participated in leadership training at work, an experience that changed her life in many ways and, unbeknownst to her, was part of the formula that would open up new opportunities in the coming years. She was presented with an opportunity in her church to work with women 1:1, then eventually to lead a group study.

That invitation unlocked within her a passion for helping women walk from a place of pain to healing and freedom, something Audrey had experienced a decade earlier.

"A friend of mine told me 12 years ago that I have a teacher inside of me. I had no idea how much I would love this." It is a gift and a passion Audrey didn't realize would become such a fulfilling part of her life.

Audrey believes the timing of this new opportunity has paired perfectly with the season of life her family is in, especially having two sons old enough to be paying attention.

> My boys are watching me pursue my dreams and cheering me on every step. My husband is so proud. He has prayed and believed with me through every season of disappointment. Now I can barely believe this part of my life, this chapter, has come. I see the outcome in the way my work impacts people and it inspires me to do even more and dream bigger.

Audrey's dream today is unlocking dreams for other women.

> I started thinking about writing my book when I was 40, but it wasn't the right time. In my 50s, all the things that had been growing within me, these things came together, and it was time.
>
> We've had so much access to research and teachings as so many things came online. The buds were starting to pop out of the ground in my 50s.

Audrey also has a message for you:

> The journey is worth it, not because we're here to build a platform, but because we can change the lives of others so deeply when we do what God has designed us to do. And be open to the new chapters that unfold with every season.

Audrey will be publishing a book and launching a podcast series: *Unlocked: Uncovering the Hidden Roots that Lock You*.

You can connect with Audrey at Godser.ky@gmail.com

## Karen Rigney, Age 63

*From hair dresser to a career in the law enforcement field in her 40s to a new career in real estate in her 60s.*

> I really am "reignited!" I love it when I learn new things and can serve others with the newfound skills. It uplifts my spirits. I really love serving and using my skills, knowledge, and experience motivates me to keep going.

Karen's adult-life journey started out fairly typical. She was married for more than 30 years to her first husband and they raised five children. Karen owned a beauty salon and did hair and nails. Karen said, "My clients were almost all in law enforcement and they encouraged me to follow suit so I would have benefits and a retirement. At 44 years old I did it and worked in the field until I was about 58."

She continued, "I retired for 'some reason' suddenly and I am glad I listened to that little voice. My husband and I both retired and relocated to Arizona. He died a year later of pancreatic cancer. I was thankful I listened and got the last year with just him."

Following her husband's death, Karen floundered for a while then met and married her retired CHP Officer husband.

Karen shared,

> We have had quite a ride. We worked a part time side job together for many years transporting high-risk youth to treatment centers, traveling all over the states, day and night. We eventually sold both of our Arizona homes, relocated to Idaho, built a house, and bought a travel trailer. We loved our

> new life together, then my husband got sick. He is doing fine now, but he moves way slower than before. We had to stop transporting and slow down our lifestyle.

Karen found herself bored in her new caretaker role. She said, "I have always led a very active life and wanted to try my hand at real estate. My husband supported me and sponsored my schooling. Now I am loving the fast-paced learning curve." She added, "I am reignited!"

She's also loving this stage in her life:

> I love being an older person; my perspectives keep changing. I want less now, much less. I long for socializing with others but not the type you might think. I don't long for cocktail or dinner parties or spending weeks out of my life traveling just to see family. We took a few weeks and went on a cruise with friends our age for the holidays. It was amazing. And I long for a purpose fulfilled by helping others meet their needs.

Karen, deservedly so, has become more selfish with the time she and her husband have together. I love that she added, "We have found sweet ways of saying no."

Karen is available at dig2dye@yahoo.com.

## Cindy Warner, 59

*Reignited her "young girl" horse dream 40 years later at age 53.*

Cindy was a little girl who loved horses.

When she was 13 years old, her horse dream started to become a reality when her parents signed her up for horseback riding lessons. But, before long, she struggled with an allergic reaction that put the brakes on her dream.

Cindy went on with her life, and a few years later, she turned her attention to tooling up for her adult life. She earned a bachelor's degree in marketing and started her professional career as a corporate recruiter. From there, with the intensity of the Type A personality that she is, she overachieved. She built a successful career that spanned decades.

Like many women, though, Cindy has a story that is not as easy as "happily ever after." Here is a portion of her story, as she tells it in her book:

> I spent most of my career 'getting it done.' I was always very dutiful—responsible, engaged, and dedicated. I focused on doing a good job, making enough money, and investing it correctly to retire at a desirable age. I bought the most efficient car, the house that was the best real estate investment, and stayed current on fashion. I got the right haircut, clothes, and makeup to fit perfectly into my organization, and I dressed for success—you know, one level higher than you are, so you are positioning yourself to be promoted.

> Yep, I did all that. I stayed up on the latest technology and traveled the world teaching leaders to manage performance, handle conflict, give feedback, present with confidence, and do strategic planning.
>
> Then one day it all fell apart. I was fired.
>
> My heart and the world I had built imploded. It almost killed me. I slowly rebuilt my life with more humility and more fear. Humbled, embarrassed, and devastated, I recovered slowly and crawled my way back to corporate America, eventually becoming a successful individual contributor again.
>
> I built a career focused on training and development, eventually running leadership development programs across the globe. I got several credentials in organizational development, leadership development, and executive coaching, and proceeded to coach and develop leaders around the world.
>
> I noticed many of them struggled to combine their analytical and business skills with their emotions and their courage of convictions. Many of them were like me: They had tremendous heart, but they had to learn how to integrate it with their analytical skills and their need to get things done quickly and well. Soon after this, I realized my life was going by with the trappings of success, but little true joy.

One day, her mom mentioned that children often outgrow allergies later in life. "I decided it was time to return to a dream I had since I was a little girl, and to make the dream come true."

In 2014, Cindy's life changed forever. She found her beautiful horse, Echo, and they get along beautifully—with no sneezing or watery eyes.

During Cindy's career, she worked with hundreds of leaders around the world who struggled to combine clear business logic, emotionally intelligent connection, and a courageous results focus—all required to become great leaders. And through all of her work, she continued to seek a more effective way to help them pull it all together.

> Echo was the "spark" who taught me how to do that, with astonishing efficiency and deep effectiveness. I had no choice! My life-changing experience with Echo inspired the "wild-ass dream" to bring this magical "horse wisdom" to the leaders who, like me, needed to learn to integrate clarity, connection and courage.
>
> I mentioned this dream to a friend, and she encouraged me to explore equine-assisted coaching programs. I sought out—and found—a coaching certification program that integrates equine-assisted coaching so I could bring this "horse wisdom" to leaders in corporate America.

Cindy became certified and has incorporated equine-assisted coaching into her business.

While Cindy's business expands beyond this specialty, the stories and concepts of horse wisdom are in everything she does. Bringing the "horse wisdom" of clarity, connection and courage is the heart of her message and her work. Cindy partners with Echo and his friends frequently to help her clients learn and practice in real time how to integrate business logic, results focus, and emotional intelligence. The work is transformational.

She took a huge leap of faith to pursue her passion and follow a dream she had long abandoned.

I asked Cindy what happened with horses between the ages of 13 and 53 when she got Echo. She said, "Nothing. Absolutely nothing."

Your dreams are never too old to reignite.

You can learn more about Cindy's services and order a copy of her book, *"Leading with Clarity, Connection and Courage: The Secret to Whole Leadership"* at cwarnercoach.com.

## What's Your Story?

As you read these stories, did you pick up some inspiration? Did something trigger an idea for you?

If so, write it down now. This is the time to capture those ideas.

As you read the stories, you may have noticed that each woman's journey unfolded naturally. You don't need to force something to happen in your life right now, but you do need to be aware that you are capable of so much—and you have opportunities ahead in your life.

**Reflection Questions**

What ideas did the stories in this chapter spark for you?

What is something you would do if you could?

What childhood dream(s) have you abandoned?

What is still holding you back from your past that you need to overcome?

## Chapter Highlights

**Chapter 1: Is There More to Life Than This?**

- Get clear about what is nagging at you, feels unresolved, and needs your attention.

**Chapter 2: Let's Get a Few Things Straight**

- You have a runway ahead of you for the second half of your life and can change your beliefs about what lies ahead.

**Chapter 3: The Sparks Have Dimmed**

- Many mid-life women experience apathy. You can treasure the memories in your positive bucket and do the work to leave the negative bucket of memories behind.

**Chapter 4: Clean Up the Things That Matter to You**

- When you look around, what do you notice? As you assess ten areas of your life, what areas need to be cleaned up? Which need to be reignited and reinvented?

**Chapter 5: Women Who Took Action to Clean Up the Mess**

- A bridge connects the old land to the new land. You don't have to have a clear picture of your new land to step onto the bridge.

**Chapter 6: It's Time to Reignite and Reinvent**

- You may very well have three, four, or five decades left, and you have a choice to settle for where you're at, reignite or reinvent.

**Chapter 7: Design Your 80-Year Old Self**

- Envision a lovely woman you know who is in her 80s, and think about your own 80-year-old self.

**Chapter 8: Inspiration From Women in Their 70s, 80s, and 90s**

- You can be fully alive in the later years of your life.

**Chapter 9: Believe in Yourself**

- Belief precedes action, Your belief in yourself is determined by you.

**Chapter 10: Transform Yourself for Action**

- Acknowledge that you have time and create a vision for your future. Then, get ready.

**Chapter 11: Get Started. Where Are YOU Going?**

- Move through the six stages of your Success Path, from assessing your starting point to navigating toward your amazing future self.

**Chapter 12: Women Who Are Doing It**

- You can get your spark back.
- Unrealized dreams can be revisited and reignited.
- You can rediscover your confidence.
- You can find greater happiness.
- Your undiscovered purpose still has time to be unleashed.

# PART V

## KEEP THE FIRE BURNING

# CHAPTER 13

## It's Time to Take Yourself Seriously

*You must do the things you think you cannot do.*

~ Eleanor Roosevelt

It's time to talk about taking yourself seriously. Why? Because it doesn't matter if you have the best of intentions, you won't be able to reignite or reinvent your life until you recognize what's at stake.

Many times, women feel guilty about doing things for themselves because it seems selfish, but what they're missing is exactly how influential they are in their own worlds. There are people all around you waiting to be inspired by what you're going to do when you implement the plans you create as you go through this book. In order to do that, you need to start taking yourself seriously.

Can you imagine going to work and not bothering to do any of the tasks you're responsible for? What if your boss didn't care enough to intervene? How long would the company stay afloat? The truth is, we owe it to ourselves—and the people we love—to take our career, personal, and financial lives seriously. We'll reap the benefits in more ways than we can predict in the decades to come.

## Be Life Rich

Ultimately, I want you to experience a rich life—now and in the future. A couple of years ago, I read *The Latte Factor*, by David Bach. The subtitle of the book is *Why You Don't Have to be Rich to Live Rich.* Bach has written numerous books to help us manage our finances. His newest title, *The Latte Factor,* covers the fundamentals that have anchored so many of his previous books: 1) pay yourself first and 2) make it automatic. In this book, he adds his third secret: "Live Rich Now."[9] I'm on board with that concept!

What does it mean to "Live Rich Now" or to "Be Life Rich"?

It means you will:

- connect with the things that bring you joy.
- be intentional.
- create joy.
- live without regrets.
- wake up every day and enjoy the moments.

- know *you're good* at the end of your life.

I want you to take time right now to pause and think about those points above. Imagine life 20, 30, or 40 years into the future. Imagine that your time is running out. You know you're close to the end of your life. Are you satisfied with what you accomplished? Did you work on the things that mattered most? Did you step out of your comfort zone often enough? Did you live life fully? Did you show up filled up each day?

The time to take yourself seriously is now. Choose to dedicate yourself to living in a way that will allow you to answer the questions above satisfactorily. Commit to do the work and become uncomfortable. Push yourself to stretch beyond momentary comfort and pleasure. Push yourself to learn, eliminate bad habits, launch new and healthy habits, delay gratification, accept fear, and do everything you can to live your life fully alive.

Decades from now I want you to be able to tell yourself:

- *I'm satisfied with my life.*
- *When I wake up each day, I'm thrilled with what lies ahead.*
- *I love what I'm doing.*
- *I love what I'm accomplishing.*
- *I'm happy with who I am.*
- *I'm confident in who I am.*

Keep in mind, this process is not supposed to be easy and comfortable every day. You have to do the work to get to your next level. You have to do the work to make your dreams come true. It's hard.

**You have to do the work to get to your next level. You have to do the work to make your dreams come true. It's hard.**

A few years ago, I was part of a panel of speakers. We were sharing ideas with our audience for how to engage and inspire their workforce.

One of the speakers shared,

> I travel to visit clients. I spend hours in my car. And for years I listened to music. It was relaxing and enjoyable. One day I arrived at my destination, turned off the car, and had a realization: I was no smarter two hours later than I was when I pulled out of my driveway.

He continued, "I started to listen to podcasts, and a whole new world opened up for me. During the same amount of time, I was now learning. It was fascinating."

I loved that idea. He inspired me to start listening to podcasts. The ideas and action steps sparked from what I learned by changing that small habit have helped shape my life and career.

Listening to experts in a variety of fields opened up a world of information.

I now listen to podcasts and YouTube videos every day: while I drive, walk, cook, fold laundry, garden, and float in the little pool in my backyard. It's part of my dedication to living my life fully. It's also how I'm taking my purpose to support *you* seriously.

Are you taking yourself seriously?

Take a look at the checklist below to see where you're at:

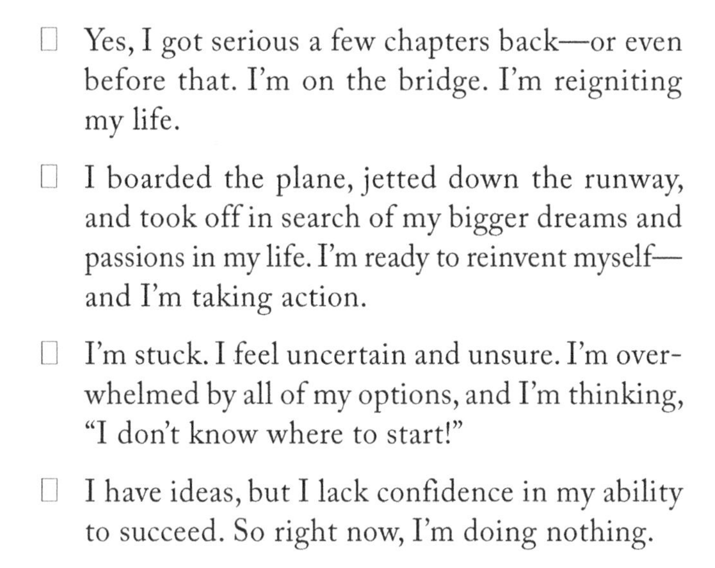

- ☐ Yes, I got serious a few chapters back—or even before that. I'm on the bridge. I'm reigniting my life.
- ☐ I boarded the plane, jetted down the runway, and took off in search of my bigger dreams and passions in my life. I'm ready to reinvent myself—and I'm taking action.
- ☐ I'm stuck. I feel uncertain and unsure. I'm overwhelmed by all of my options, and I'm thinking, "I don't know where to start!"
- ☐ I have ideas, but I lack confidence in my ability to succeed. So right now, I'm doing nothing.

If you're on the bridge or jetting off in the direction of your dreams, I'm doing cartwheels for you!

If you're stuck, I'd like to encourage you. You can do this. Start with one small step. Choose one area of your life to make progress in. Don't overthink this. Start by doing one small thing.

If you lack confidence, I understand. Perhaps you've been beat down by others, made to feel that you don't matter, or that you're a failure.

Let me remind you again: you are not your past.

You are not what other people tell you. You are amazing. And you have the ability—and the right—to create a life you can feel excited about and proud of.

**I know so many women who are living lives that feel unfulfilling. It doesn't have to be that way.**

It's time to get serious about yourself, your life, your happiness, your confidence, and your clarity of purpose.

I know so many women who are living lives that feel unfulfilling. It doesn't have to be that way.

What about you? Are you unfulfilled?

And, listen, it qualifies if you say, "I'm not unhappy, but I'm also not truly happy."

You. Deserve. More.

Are you ready? From the list below, check all that apply.

- ☐ Yes, I am ready to take myself seriously.
- ☐ I may not know exactly what to do, but I am ready.
- ☐ I am ready to grow into a belief in myself.
- ☐ I am ready to put myself first.
- ☐ I am ready to unlock doors to things I never knew existed.
- ☐ I am ready to do the work.
- ☐ I am ready to step out of my comfort zone.
- ☐ I am ready to live life fully.
- ☐ I am ready to show up filled up every day.
- ☐ I agree, I deserve more.

## Let's Get Real About the Tough Stuff:

I have a friend who is amazing in so many ways.

But there is an area of her life that needs action. It needs her serious attention. It needs her to take herself seriously.

It's an area of her life that she needs to reignite. I could go so far as to say she wants to reinvent this part of her life.

And it's difficult.

Each time I talk to her, she tells me something about the deep sadness she struggles with due to the weight she's gained.

She feels depressed.

She has lost confidence.

She hates getting dressed in the morning.

She is embarrassed when she goes out with her friends.

She hates (yes, hates) dress shopping for special occasions.

Now, mind you, she is a beautiful person. Yes, she is a larger woman. But—yes, I said "but"—she is beautiful. Stunning, in fact.

She is also sad, discouraged, and exasperated.

I talked to her about this struggle one day. I asked, "Should we talk about some ideas?" She emphatically said, "Yes!"

"What would you think about making sure you don't eat for a solid 12 hours from evening to morning?" I asked.

She said, "I don't think I could do that since I work so late, and we always have a lot of food in the breakroom."

"What would you think about eating only one helping of food at lunch and dinner instead of two?

She said, "I don't think I could do that. I'd still be hungry?"

"What would you think about no longer eating sugar?" I asked.

"I could never do that."

I asked, "Could you give up chips, crackers, cookies, cake, and candy?"

"I don't think so."

"What would you like to do differently?"

"I don't know. It's all so hard."

Can you see yourself in this story?

We all have something that's incredibly hard. But I want you to know what I told my friend: "It's not supposed to be easy."

If weight loss were easy, 60% of women would not report feeling self-conscious about their appearance.

If starting a business were easy, more women would fulfill their lifelong dream of having their own business.

If finding—or retooling for—a new career were easy, more women would leave unfulfilling jobs.

Change, improvement, growth, and advocating for yourself to have an amazing life—all of these things require hard work.

But I also want you to remember this: you can do this! You are worth every bit of work it will take to make your wishes and dreams come true.

## Chapter Highlights

**Chapter 1: Is There More to Life Than This?**

- Get clear about what is nagging at you, feels unresolved, and needs your attention.

**Chapter 2: Let's Get a Few Things Straight**

- You have a runway ahead of you for the second half of your life and can change your beliefs about what lies ahead.

**Chapter 3: The Sparks Have Dimmed**

- Many mid-life women experience apathy. You can treasure the memories in your positive bucket and do the work to leave the negative bucket of memories behind.

**Chapter 4: Clean Up the Things That Matter to You**

- When you look around, what do you notice? As you assess ten areas of your life, what areas need to be cleaned up? Which need to be reignited and reinvented?

**Chapter 5: Women Who Took Action to Clean Up the Mess**

- A bridge connects the old land to the new land. You don't have to have a clear picture of your new land to step onto the bridge.

**Chapter 6: It's Time to Reignite and Reinvent**

- You may very well have three, four or five decades left, and you have a choice to settle for where you're at, reignite or reinvent.

**Chapter 8: Inspiration From Women in Their 70s, 80s, and 90s**

- You can be fully alive in the later years of your life.

**Chapter 7: Design Your 80-Year Old Self**

- Envision a lovely woman you know who is in her 80s, and think about your own 80-year-old self.

**Chapter 9: Believe in Yourself**

- Belief precedes action. Your belief in yourself is determined by you.

**Chapter 10: Transform Yourself for Action**

- Acknowledge that you have time, and create a vision for your future. Then, get ready.

**Chapter 11: Get Started. Where Are YOU Going?**

- Move through the six stages of your success path, from assessing your starting point to navigating toward your amazing future self.

**Chapter 12: Women Who Are Doing It**

- Your undiscovered purpose still has time to be unleashed. You can get your spark back.

**Chapter 13: It's Time to Get Serious**

- Be life rich.
- It's time to take yourself seriously.
- It's not supposed to be easy.
- Are you ready to do that work required to reignite and reinvent your life?

# CHAPTER 14

## BRING ON THE CONFIDENCE

*"Believe in yourself. Have faith in your abilities! Without a humble but reasonable confidence in your own powers, you cannot be successful or happy."*

~ Norman Vincent Peale

How would having more confidence change your life? How would you feel? What would you do differently? I want you to have a crystal clear picture of why you want to be more confident because it's completely achievable—but it's going to take some serious work.

I know you were born with the innate ability to be confident. It was illustrated over and over again before you even reached kindergarten. Have you ever thought about what it took for you to learn how to walk? How many times did you fall down? Why did you keep getting up? What made you confident you could walk when you had never done it before?

The perseverance and grit that got you through your childhood can continue to help you build confidence at any age.

Although this is a book for women, I'd like to share a list of men who can serve as inspiration. Each person below must have channeled an incredible amount of confidence through years of failure—and it sure paid off:

- Howard Schultz, the founder of Starbucks, went to 242 banks in his attempt to secure a loan. He was finally given a loan by individual investors.
- Thomas Edison had more than 1,000 failed attempts before he successfully created an electric light bulb.
- Walt Disney was told Mickey Mouse would fail.
- Colonel Sanders started KFC at age 60, investing his first social security check. He worked from age 60–73 to master his technique then sold his company for $2 million.
- Before Abraham Lincoln was elected as president in 1860, he lost his job, was defeated for state legislature, failed in his business, had a nervous breakdown, was defeated running for speaker of the house, was defeated after being nominated for congress, lost another nomination for congress, was defeated running for US Senate, was defeated running for Vice President, and was defeated running for US Senate.

Success isn't supposed to come easy. And your confidence will be tested multiple times along the way.

It's likely your journey will be filled with moments when you think:

- *I can't do this.*
- *This is too hard.*
- *Who do I think I am?*
- *What was I thinking?*
- *They were right.*

I'm here to tell you something:

- You *can* do this.
- You *can* persevere.
- You *can*, with hard work, make it to the finish line.
- You *can* push through your fears.
- You *can* achieve your goals.
- Your dreams *can* come true.

I want to tell you about my friend, Dr. Colleen Georges. In 2019, she released her book, *"Rescript the Story You're Telling Yourself: The Eight Practices to Quiet your Inner Antagonist, Amplify Your Inner Advocate & Author a Limitless Life."*[10] We became friends when I ordered her book, propped it on my shelf, took a photo of it, and sent it to her.

I struck the lottery when I met her.

Dr. Colleen has become a valued expert guest speaker in my *Accountability and Friendship for Success* membership community.

She drew me in when she shared her book-writing journey. She explained, "I started writing a book in 2003, wrote 17 pages and stopped. My Inner Antagonist kept telling me it was too late, and I let myself believe it."

More than a decade later, she started writing again.

> I was going strong writing. I got about 40 pages in, and all of a sudden, the Inner Antagonists' voice resurfaced. It whispered at first, but eventually it got louder. It said writing was too much and I couldn't handle it. It said I didn't have time. It said working to make money was the more important priority. Eventually, I let myself believe it, again. And I stopped, again.

Later, following an invitation to do a TEDx Talk, Dr. Colleen unleashed a new idea related to the stories we tell ourselves. The net outcome of this part of her journey is that it gave her clarity about her book, and it gave her the confidence to make her dream come true, the dream of writing a self-growth book to empower others, the dream that had been with her for nearly three decades.

She quieted her Inner Antagonist—the part of us who tells us we can't do things—and amplified her Inner Advocate—the part of us who tells us we can. And she wrote an award-winning book.

I know you are managing the relationship between your Inner Antagonist and your Inner Advocate. We all are.

Just as Dr. Colleen teaches, you can quiet your Inner Antagonist. You can amplify your Inner Advocate.

The world needs whatever it is that is percolating inside of you. It needs you at your best. We need you at your best. Clean up the things that need to be cleaned up, then lean into that vision of your amazing future self.

Be ready to wake up every day poised to make progress.

Do something.

Every day.

Are you looking for the confidence to make this happen?

## Confidence is a Skill, Not a Trait

Many women go through their lives claiming they simply don't have confidence. I understand. Some women display innate confidence as young girls and are able to maintain that. Other women experienced their confidence wane during their formative years. Or they've never experienced a feeling of confidence at all.

Research has shown that young girls begin to lose their confidence by age 10 or 11. Of the hundreds of women I've surveyed, 25% checked the box that said, "I have no confidence." Many of these women also say, "Mean things said by others have caused my lack of confidence."

It doesn't have to be this way.

Confidence is a skill, something you can develop. How? Well, it's not about standing in front of the mirror and telling yourself that you're great. No, building confidence takes hard work. And, that's a good thing, because if you simply stood in front of the mirror, you probably wouldn't believe yourself.

Instead, I'm going to share five ways you can build more confidence through skills that result in better outcomes in life. Some might surprise you, but I'm positive you'll love where you end up if you embrace this approach:

1. **Plan to persevere.**

   By now, you know life doesn't always go as planned. But you can be mentally ready to persevere through any challenge. Unexpected problems can threaten your confidence, but knowing you will face every difficulty head on with a "won't quit" attitude will set you up for success. And the more times you work through something difficult, the more your confidence will grow. After all, you have practice dealing with anything life throws your way.

   **By now, you know life doesn't always go as planned. But you can be mentally ready to persevere through any challenge**

2. **Put time limits on your fear.**

   You will worry. Will this work? What will people think? What if I fail? If you find yourself starting to worry, give yourself time. Grab your journal and write down everything you're worried about. Then for each item, write a response. When you plan time to worry, you give yourself permission to get your problems out of your head and onto paper. Once you have them written down you can see what you're dealing with and whether there's something you need to be doing rather than merely worrying.

3. **Work through confusion.**

   Boy, oh boy, oh boy, oh boy. Have I ever been confused in the past 18 months. I don't believe I can list out all of the things I've had to learn about while creating an online business to help women spark.

Following a 30-year career where I've enjoyed a level of expertise, I ventured into unknown territory.

I've had moments where I feel despair. Overwhelmed. A feeling of, "How will I ever understand this?" "This is too hard." "This is too confusing."

But here's the thing, I know that if I'm *not* confused, I'm *not* growing.

Life has been changing incredibly fast for the past couple of centuries. And it's going to keep changing in the years we have left. We need to get used to confusion—and keep working through it.

**If you feel your confidence takes a hit every time you feel confused, it's time to change how you think about confusion.**

If you feel your confidence takes a hit every time you feel confused, it's time to change how you think about confusion. Get comfortable with working through it. Nothing can stop you if you choose to keep going.

4. **Keep learning.**

This is the perfect next step to follow the whole thing about confusion. Wake up every day ready to learn something new. As I mentioned earlier, starting an online business was intimidating. My confidence wavered along the way, but I dug in. Learning is possible at any age.

Want to know another thing, though? Structure is a key ingredient. I learned that I need to approach a confusing situation as if I'm taking a class in school.

I need to schedule time to work through it—even though it's self-directed. If you're struggling to persevere, consider scheduling the time needed and break through the confusion by learning what you don't already know.

5. **Develop mental toughness.**

The culmination of everything else is mental toughness. You will need this time and time again.

When you're tempted to relax—when taking the next necessary step is not really what you want to do—demonstrate the mental toughness to do the work anyway. It's going to be worth it to make progress toward reigniting an area of your life that is suffering or to move in the direction of your dream.

When someone says something that casts doubt, persevere. Push through it and keep going.

When the voices in your own head are telling you that you can't do something, rise above those thoughts.

When you're tired and you want to kick back and have a glass of wine with your girlfriends, stay on track. If your dream is a big one, make progress every single day.

If you've come home from your day job and you want to make progress—but you're exhausted and can think of nothing better than plopping on the couch with the remote control in your hand—just Grab 15. Set a timer and do something for 15 minutes.

Get tough and you *will* get confident.

## Let's Get Real About the Tough Stuff

Jennifer McCune, who is my Rodan + Fields rep, is the embodiment of confidence—and her story is proof that confidence can be built one difficult call at a time.

She has been running a home-based business for more than eight years—so successfully that she is a Premier Level V Mercedes Benz Achiever. Now, I don't know what a Premier Level V is, but I do know what a Mercedes Benz is. Jennifer knows what she's doing.

I've interacted with her many times, and I know her to be a confident, assertive business owner and service provider. She stayed in the game and worked persistently—though very respectfully—to win me as a customer. Well over a year.

I asked Jennifer, "When you started your business, did you ever struggle?" Her reply, "Oh my gosh, are you kidding me? I thought I was going to die every time I made a phone call. I prayed that women wouldn't answer their phones so I could simply leave a message."

She also added that she could feel her friends looking down on her. Jennifer, who earned a Ph.D. and worked at a regular job before starting her own company—McCune Health and Wellness, LLC—believes her friends saw that as a sign she wasn't succeeding in her profession.

As the CEO of her organization, Jennifer leads and mentors the women who have dreams of replicating her success.

Jennifer is an example of the success we can experience when we persevere, allow worry to have its proper place, accept confusion as part of the journey, learn in order to tackle the confusion head-on, and develop a mental toughness that leads us to our ultimate success.

Today, knowing Jennifer as I do, I can hear her thinking as she makes her phone calls, "Please pick up!" She is an enjoyable conversationalist and an inspiring representative of her product line. I'm sold!

## Chapter Highlights

**Chapter 1: Is There More to Life Than This?**

- Get clear about what is nagging at you, feels unresolved, and needs your attention.

**Chapter 2: Let's Get a Few Things Straight**

- You have a runway ahead of you for the second half of your life and can change your beliefs about what lies ahead.

**Chapter 3: The Sparks Have Dimmed**

- Many mid-life women experience apathy. You can treasure the memories in your positive bucket and do the work to leave the negative bucket of memories behind.

**Chapter 4: Clean Up the Things That Matter to You**

- When you look around, what do you notice? As you assess ten areas of your life, what areas need to be cleaned up? Which need to be reignited and reinvented?

**Chapter 5: Women Who Took Action to Clean Up the Mess**

- A bridge connects the old land to the new land. You don't have to have a clear picture of your new land to step onto the bridge.

**Chapter 6: It's Time to Reignite and Reinvent**

- You may very well have three, four or five decades left, and you have a choice to settle for where you're at, reignite or reinvent.

**Chapter 7: Design Your 80-Year Old Self**

- Envision a lovely woman you know who is in her 80s, and think about your own 80-year-old self.

**Chapter 8: Inspiration From Women in Their 70s, 80s, and 90s**

- You can be fully alive in the later years of your life.

**Chapter 9: Believe in Yourself**

- Belief precedes action. Your belief in yourself is determined by you.

**Chapter 10: Transform Yourself for Action**

- Acknowledge that you have time and create a vision for your future. Then, get ready.

**Chapter 11: Get Started. Where Are YOU Going?**

- Move through the six stages of your success path, from assessing your starting point to navigating toward your amazing future self.

**Chapter 12: Women Who Are Doing It**

- Your undiscovered purpose still has time to be unleashed. You can get your spark back.

**Chapter 13: It's Time to Get Serious**

- Be life rich. Are you ready to do the work required to reignite and reinvent your life?

**Chapter 14: Bring on the Confidence**

- Get back up as many times as you fall down.
- Your confidence will be tested.
- Your Inner Antagonist will tell you that you can't. Your Inner Advocate will tell you that you can.
- Remember you can!
- Develop your confidence skill.
- Plan to persevere.
- Put time limits on your fear.
- Work through confusion.
- Keep learning.
- Develop mental toughness.

# CHAPTER 15

## YOUR BRIDGES AND RUNWAYS

*"Life is not easy for any of us. But what of that? We must have perseverance and above all confidence in ourselves. We must believe that we are gifted for something and that this thing must be attained."*

~ Marie Curie

I wrote this book because I want to encourage and inspire you to reignite or reinvent your life for an amazing second half.

I hope you are encouraged and inspired.

I hope you're ready to do more and be more.

And, finally, I hope you rest confident in the belief that you *can* both do more and be more—if that is what you want.

We've covered a lot of ground.
Let's review:

1. You've read stories of many women who, just like you, have navigated through the ups and downs of life. You've learned how they reignited and reinvented their lives.
2. You've thought about the things that are nagging at you.
3. You've contemplated the two, three, or four-decades-long runway ahead of you.
4. You've thought about the things in your life you'd like to leave behind.
5. You've considered the ten areas of your life and what needs to be cleaned up.
6. You've envisioned your 80-year old self and created a picture of what she's doing.
7. You've planned your success path across the bridge and off the runway.
8. You've learned how to transform yourself for action.

Nice work in making it all the way to the end of this book. That's a big accomplishment. That means something.

Now it's time to put what you've learned to work for you in your life.

Perhaps you've already started. Your copy of this book may be filled with highlights, underlined passages, and margin notes. Or, maybe it's your journal that you've filled up. It's also possible you prefer to read through a book like this one time to capture the essence—and then you go back to do the work.

Whatever your approach, I am here rooting for you and cheering you on!

## What Are You Ready For?

By now, you likely know what you're ready for. The wheels are spinning.

Before you make any final decisions about what you're ready for today, I want you to think ahead. Think about one year from now. How about five years from now? And ten? Imagine you are essentially doing nothing differently. Your health is the same (or worse), your home hasn't changed, your friendships still feel "meh," you don't have any hobbies or interests of your own, you're still working in a career you're not as thrilled about as you once were, and you're even more in debt than you are now.

Yes, imagine all that.

Do you want things to be the same one, five, or ten years from now? Do you want to be feeling the same level of restlessness or dissatisfaction or lack of spark in your life?

And remember your 80-year old self? What progress are you making to ensure she's firing on all cylinders?

I hope this reality check will spur you into action.

As you look at the options below, check the one that most resonates with you today:

- ☐ I have some cleaning up to do in my day-to-day life. I'm going to step onto the bridge, identify the areas of my life that I'd like to improve, and reignite my spark.

- ☐ I'm ready to make progress on my passion projects, my bigger purpose in life, and my next chapter. I know it's time to head to the runway, take off toward a new future, and reinvent myself for the second half.
- ☐ Both for me!

## What's Next?

Think about your bridges and runways.

Are you on the bridge? Are you exploring the portions of your life where you may be feeling dissatisfaction and discouragement?

Are you on the runway, making progress to your bigger dreams?

Maybe both! This is not uncommon. Lots of women are juggling improvements in their day-to-day lives while also advancing their bigger dreams and passions.

Regardless of which area you plan to work on first, progress is made one step at a time. Just one.

**Regardless of which area you plan to work on first, progress is made one step at a time. Just one.**

Create your master list, decide what's first for you, and start to make progress. One step at a time. One day at a time.

When you make progress every single day, big and wonderful things are bound to happen for you.

## Do You Want to Dig Deeper?

I hope so!

If you'd like to bring this book—and your journey—to life, I have three ideas for you:

1. Begin to create your plan in an organized, step-by-step way. Download a free copy of the *Women Who Spark* SPARK Planner at www.aletanorris.com/sparkplanner.
2. If you'd like a guided journey through this book with a community of women doing the same thing, video lessons for added inspiration, and weekly group coaching calls for added friendly accountability, sign up (or join the waitlist) for *Women Who Spark* Midlife Makeover at www.aletanorris.com/midlifemakeover. Midlife Makeover is an eight-week journey that I host in the spring and fall.
3. Join my monthly membership community, *Accountability and Friendship for Success (AFS).* This is an amazing community of women who have put a stake in the ground to make steady progress in their lives for—well, forever. As a member of AFS, you receive a variety of benefits: weekly email nudges, weekly coaching sessions, purely social virtual gatherings, speakers, challenges—and more, all designed to help women make steady progress over time. You can learn more at www.aletanorris.com/AFSMembership.

Your future is important! Don't leave this journey across the bridge to chance. Join the Women Who Spark Community for added support, accountability and inspiration. I hope we'll see you soon!

### Chapter Highlights

**Chapter 1: Is There More to Life Than This?**

- Get clear about what is nagging at you, feels unresolved, and needs your attention.

**Chapter 2: Let's Get a Few Things Straight**

- You have a runway ahead of you for the second half of your life and can change your beliefs about what lies ahead.

**Chapter 3: The Sparks Have Dimmed**

- Many mid-life women experience apathy. You can treasure the memories in your positive bucket and do the work to leave the negative bucket of memories behind.

**Chapter 4: Clean Up the Things That Matter to You**

- When you look around, what do you notice? As you assess ten areas of your life, what areas need to be cleaned up? Which need to be reignited and reinvented?

**Chapter 5: Women Who Took Action to Clean Up the Mess**

- A bridge connects the old land to the new land. You don't have to have a clear picture of your new land to step onto the bridge.

**Chapter 6: It's Time to Reignite and Reinvent**

- You may very well have three, four or five decades left, and you have a choice to settle for where you're at, reignite or reinvent.

**Chapter 7: Design Your 80-Year Old Self**

- Envision a lovely woman you know who is in her 80s, and think about your own 80-year-old self.

**Chapter 8: Inspiration From Women in Their 70s, 80s, and 90s**

- You can be fully alive in the later years of your life.

**Chapter 9: Believe in Yourself**

- Belief precedes action. Your belief in yourself is determined by you.

**Chapter 10: Transform Yourself for Action**

- Acknowledge that you have time and create a vision for your future. Then, get ready.

**Chapter 11: Get Started. Where Are YOU Going?**

- Move through the six stages of your success path, from assessing your starting point to navigating toward your amazing future self.

**Chapter 12: Women Who Are Doing It**

- Your undiscovered purpose still has time to be unleashed. You can get your spark back.

**Chapter 13: It's Time to Get Serious**

- Be life rich. Are you ready to do the work required to reignite and reinvent your life?

**Chapter 14: Bring on the Confidence**

- Develop your confidence.

**Chapter 15: Your Bridges and Runways**

- What are you ready for?
    - Are you on the bridge, exploring portions of your life where you may be feeling dissatisfied?
    - Are you on the runway, making progress toward bigger dreams?
- Do you want to dig deeper?
    - Download your SPARK planner at www.aletanorris.com/sparkplanner
    - Join Midlife Makeover at www.aletanorris.com/midlifemakeover.
    - Join the monthly membership community, Accountability and Friendship for Success at www.aletanorris.com/AFSMembership.

## Where do you go from here?

Reading this book is a starting point. As you move forward, I would love to remain part of your support team.

Please visit my website at aletanorris.com to find out how to stay in touch.

- You can join my *Women Who Spark Tribe* Facebook Community at www.facebook.com/groups/womenwhospark
- Sign up for my *Women Who Spark Midlife Makeover* at www.aletanorris.com/midlifemakeover
- Join my Membership community, *Accountability and Friendship for Success,* at www.aletanorris.com/AFSMembership
- Drop me a line at aleta@aletanorris.com.

Please let me know how I can help you, my friend.

Aleta xo

## *Women Who Spark* Midlife Makeover

Join an eight-week guided journey of this book. Midlife Makeover is an interactive, online experience, designed to help you reinvent and reignite your life for the second half!

**What will you experience?**

- Eight weeks of content, including 30 video lessons, with a workbook to track your progress
- Small group coaching support
- A roadmap for your amazing future, by creating your own SPARK Plan
- Camaraderie with other women on the exact same journey

Learn more at www.aletanorris.com/midlifemakeover

## *Women Who Spark* Accountability and Friendship for Success

I am so excited about this amazing membership community.

Are you looking for an accountability group, one filled with like-minded women striving for their own amazing future? Is friendship something that is important to you?

Accountability and Friendship for Success (AFS) is a membership community designed for women in midlife, women who want to cross the bridge to the new land—a land of greater happiness, confidence and clarity of purpose.

Membership open twice a year.

**What will you experience?**

- Weekly progress nudges
- Small group coaching support
- A private Facebook community
- Monthly speakers
- Group challenges

Learn more at www.aletanorris.com/AFSMembership.

# ACKNOWLEDGMENTS

**To the Women Who Spark Tribe.** When I wrote my first book—Women Who Spark—in 2018, I had no idea how special you all would become. At that time, there were 0 of you. Today, there are thousands of you. You have come along with me and inspired me with your stories of success and struggle. Let's stay on this journey together. We have a lot of decades ahead of us.

**To my husband, Steve.** It's wonderful living with another creative in the house. Thank you for giving me the space I need write, write, write. You're my biggest cheerleader for everything, and I'm so grateful for you.

**To my amazing children, your spouses and your significant others** (Jaimie and Chris, Ben and Kelsey, Steph and Andy, Joe and Andrea, Haley and Brandon). You give me my spark. You're my greatest joy.

**To Teri Capshaw,** my talented and invaluable editor. Teri, one of the best decisions I made for *Women Who Spark After 50* was to bring you along from the very beginning—before one word was even written. Thank you for being with me all the way through book #2. Stay on deck for #3! I can't do Women Who Spark without you.

**To Author Academy Elite and the Igniting Souls Tribe.** Not every author has the backing of an amazing publishing company and a supportive group of 1000s of authors. It makes the journey enjoyable and inspirational. Thank you, Kary Oberbrunner, for creating this amazing publishing company and community.

**To all of the wonderful women featured in this book.** Thank you for sharing your stories with the women who need to hear them. I treasure your openness and vulnerability.

# ENDNOTES


1 Guise, Stephen, *Mini Habits: Smaller Habits, Bigger Results,* 2013.

2 Wu, Suzanne, "The Happiness Gap," USC Dornsife, July 1, 2008, Accessed online 08/10/20.

3 Sedlar, Jeri and Miners, Rick. *Don't Retire Rewire: 5 Steps to Fulfilling Work That Fuels your Passion, Suits Your Personality and Fills Your Pocket,* Penguin Random House, 2018.

4 Frost, Robert, "The Road Not Taken," 1916, (poetryfoundation.org)

5 Braverman, Janette, *10 Reasons Communication Brings Transformation: Unleash Your Greatness,* HenschelHaus Publishing, 2017.

6 Turley, Joan, *Sacred Work in Secular Places: Finding Joy in the Workplace,* Author Academy Elite, 2017.

[7] Elrod, Hal, *The Miracle Morning: The Not-So-Obvious Secret Guaranteed to Transform Your Life Before 8 AM,* 2018.

[8] Guise, Stephen, *Mini Habits: Smaller Habits, Bigger Results,* 2013.

[9] Bach, David. *The Latte Factor: Why You Don't Have to Be Rich to Live Rich,* Atria Books, 2019.

[10] Georges, Dr. Colleen. *Rescript the Story You're Telling Yourself: The Eight Practices to Quiet your Inner Antagonist, Amplify Your Inner Advocate & Author a Limitless Life,* Author Academy Elite, 2019.

Made in the USA
Las Vegas, NV
12 March 2023

68973396R00164